A Fascination with Forward

Why Forgiveness Matters

Deborah Candler

Order this book online at www.trafford.com
or email orders@trafford.com

Most Trafford titles are also available at major online book retailers.

Printed in the United States of America.

ISBN: 978-1-4669-9271-9 (sc)
ISBN: 978-1-4669-9272-6 (hc)
ISBN: 978-1-4669-9273-3 (e)

Library of Congress Control Number: 2013907885

Trafford rev. 05/02/2013

 www.trafford.com

North America & international
toll-free: 1 888 232 4444 (USA & Canada)
phone: 250 383 6864 ♦ fax: 812 355 4082

DEDICATION

My loved and treasured Dad—you were my hero, my mentor, my inspiration, and my friend. You stepped unexpectedly into your fullness of life just short of seeing this book in print. You were adamant that you would have the first-signed copy—that you shall have.

You were a legacy in life and in death. I am proud to carry your DNA of faith and I will to the best of my ability perpetuate what you pioneered, nurture what you invested, guard what you built, and cultivate what you sowed into my life.

You ran the race, you finished the course, you kept the faith, you received the eternal gold. Now we pick up the baton and continue the race. Knowing that our footsteps resonate into eternity, we look with future eyes to our children's, children's children knowing that when we have run our race, and passed our batons we will all be reunited in eternity on that great day.

Both my little girl and my grown woman memories hold you dear and close in my heart until that anticipated day.

. . . He has placed eternity in the hearts of His people.

Ecclesiastes 3:11

P.S.

Just prior to this book going to print, my dad was admitted to hospital with severe pain in his leg. He had been a medal winning long distance runner all his life and as recently as four years prior had received third place in the Australian Masters games in Canberra at age seventy-four.

In all his life, he had never taken medication or been ill. He had just finished building his hot house for his vegetable seedlings. Dad could build anything, fix anything, and design anything. I write these last concluding thoughts in front of the fire in the beautiful house he and mum built together, surrounded by the ten acres of trees, and natives they planted together. This is the family home where we all gather for Christmas.

He was a brilliant communicator and possessed an uncanny and unusual mind that could remember and recall information on church and world history, politics, sports, current affairs, and most strikingly for us as a family—the Word of God, or the Bible. He was our "bat stop" or "keeper" in life. We constantly deferred to him, were intrigued by, and welcomed his opinion.

His grandchildren loved and adored him and he invested enormously into each of their individual lives. His four children, their spouses, and all his nine grandchildren (and the two fiancees of the two eldest grandsons) all answered to his pet names.

Christmas and other times that brought some or all of our families together were among the richest times in life for us.

Doctors spent a week trying to stabilize the pain but to no avail. Further tests would require him to be transported to a larger hospital. But before arrangements were made, he suffered a heart attack at the end of that week which required surgery.

The pain persisted and increased. His heart arrested again at the end of the day and he was gone. We never did find out the initial cause of leg pain.

The grief was too much for us—we were unprepared, this crisis came unannounced and we were left with many questions.

Again, the forgiveness life style is put to the test.

But our Dad's DNA is etched in us and in our children, and we all in unspoken agreement chose responses that would affirm life rather than neutralize it. We have been open to explore the limits of our capacity for love and growth and are determined to propagate Dad's legacy of faith, life, and hope.

In a public memorial service, our family paid tribute to this extraordinary man who lived an extraordinary life extraordinarily well. Nine people indicated their surrender to God and ten took Bibles out of intrigue for what directed and fueled this man. (A fascination with forward perhaps?) Countless people ordered the video recording to hear the message again. These are ripples on the pond that continue to touch unknown shores.

Our pain is still fresh but so are our wonderful memories. Our loss is still great but so is our hope.

His earthly season transitioned into his eternal season but he has left a wake of blessing and his message of heritage, destiny, and eternity still resonate throughout this life.

We carry his DNA in our souls, his love in our hearts, and his memories in our minds forever.

. . . "Well done good and faithful servant; you have
been faithful over a few things, I will make you ruler over
many things. Enter into the joy of your Lord."

Matthew 25:23

THANKS

To my irresistible Philip. Was there life before you? You are the manifestation of a list, the answer to a prayer, and the love of my life. You are my joy, my laughter, and my constant encourager. Thank you for your unusual belief in me and your "whatever it takes" kind of love. Thank you for sharing your deep insight, your balanced perspective and your divine wisdom at any, and all hours throughout this creation. I am and always will be grateful for the gift of you.

To my precious sons, James and Matthew. You have taught me much about forgiving and unconditional love. Your patience, maturity, and resilience over the years have covered a multitude of mothering errors. You have courageously picked up the baton of faith, heritage, and destiny, and I could not be prouder.

To the incomparable Joy Graetz. You have gathered me among like-minded yet unlikely friends that I should be stretched, encouraged, and challenged. You have graciously encompassed me into your life and allowed me to draw from your wells of wisdom and life experience. You have encouraged me, taught me, comforted me, warned me, and championed me. Your dual gift of time and editing has been invaluable for the completing of this book. Thank you, my friend.

FOREWORD

For almost thirteen years, I have been working with CEO's and influential business leaders in Australia and abroad. I have authored intellectual property and worked on the creation of business systems that are used by a variety of people to optimize business relationships, systems, and bottom lines. During this time, I have had the privilege of meeting and working with a diverse array of clients and their partners. One meeting in particular shines in my memory as a stand out story—it's a story of serendipity and love.

It was while working with the leaders of a large Australian company based on the Gold Coast that I first met Philip Candler. Today, Phil is married to the author of this work. And let me tell you, it is no coincidence that this couple have the surname "Candler" as they are both like candlelights that stand tall and burn brightly, passing on ways for others to light their own candles. Whatever and whoever they touch becomes illuminated.

During the course of working with Phil and his colleagues, I had the honor of being privy to Phil's journey as he met, dated, and finally married an incredible woman in Deb. He began sharing snippets of the woman who had brought so much joy and happiness into his life and I became more and more curious.

As time passed and my work with this company progressed, I eventually met Deb over a business dinner. Under the dim lights of the restaurant, I recall thinking her face was illuminated, almost like she was in a spotlight. This woman, I thought, has a love inside her that is so strong and so encompassing that it is heavenly. She is a gift. The love, peace, and strength she transmits is difficult to convey in words, yet there is such a humility, purity, and gentleness all besides her physical beauty. And here we find ourselves years later linked by the invitation to read the manuscript of a book Deb had written.

I read *A Fascination with Forward* on a plane to East Africa and I didn't put it down. I have literally read hundreds of business and personal development books over the years; some good, some not so good. This book, however, is different. It has a palpable healing quality. Not a new age healing that is broad, diffuse, and hard to nail down. Not a self-actualization healing that is appealing but void of tangible truth. But a healing quality that lifts you and takes you to another place that no other self-awareness book can do. Why? Because I believe this book is founded on authentic and ancient wisdom. Its words clearly have the Spirit of God working through them. It has God's grace and the unconditional love of Christ bursting warmth and confirming truth from its pages! And if you are finally open enough to truly forgive and be forgiven, you will understand what I mean.

This is not a religious book. It is a spiritual book. It is a book on love.

So to you the reader, I challenge you to take a different journey to another part of yourself—the part that can truly love and be loved—and while there, discover your maker. You'll be amazed at what love illuminates and you'll be amazed with who you really are when forgiveness reigns. And if you get the chance to hear Deb speak or meet her, take it! But this I can assure you, once you have read this book, you will feel like you have found a friend.

If you are ready to move your life forward and if you've searched your soul and decided, it's your time to move on, then now is the right time to read this book. *A Fascination with Forward* eloquently and compassionately takes you to the deep places of healing and then releases you to live out your plan A! What this book is not, is a shallow "self-help" book. What this book is, is an unveiling of wisdom so true, so pure, so rich that it has the capacity to tear the root of your pain right out and give your heart wings.

Tanya Lacy
Intercept Coaching Systems and The Coaches Consortium.

CONTENTS

WHY
FORGIVENESS
MATTERS

WHY FORGIVENESS MATTERS

The principles found in this book will help you squeeze more joy out of your life than you thought possible! I know this because I have proved them to be right.

Somewhere between the destination (where we want to be) and the journey (where we are) is a place called stuck.

Disappointments, tragedies, heartaches, crises, mistakes, and failures (those of ourselves and of others) can consume us with negative patterns of:

- *physiology* (tone of voice, panic attacks, rash decisions);
- *language ("I'll never get back what I've lost."; "I'm too old."; "I've blown my chance."); and*
- *belief* (that we had it coming to us; that we'll never get ahead financially; that it's all too hard and not worth the fight)

Life is reduced to focusing on getting by rather than on really living. Momentum slows down to snail-paced survival as dreams are dashed and vision is snuffed out. Self honor, respect, and confidence become orphans of our soul and, after a time, we even stop hearing them vie for our attention.

I was on my way to this place called Stuck when, in my thirty-seventh year, everything changed as I allowed God's divine intelligence and higher logic to guide my life in his mysterious and loving way. He took me through my personal crises and out of "stuck."

A Fascination with Forward is a book about grace. When grace marks us, we are never quite the same. Imagine a pebble touching the waters of our heart, causing ripples to move out from us as a never-ending, gentle, consistent stream touching those around us and even those far from us.

Forgiveness is the pebble and its effects—grace—are the ripples shared in this book. I speak of forgiveness as:

- a conscious, determined process
- a struggle to implement
- a fierce battle to achieve and
- a discipline to maintain.

It would want to be worth it! Believe me it is.

I have discovered that the path to anything worthwhile is rarely well landscaped and sign posted. I have learned that dreams do not happen automatically nor is excellence effortless. Life is built on choices, not luck; on actions, not just good ideas. Different choices and actions will take us down drastically different paths.

Learning to live with an attitude of forgiveness is learning to make better choices and to implement different actions that will move us toward a more desired future. It is intentional, not accidental!

> *Forgiveness is very different to merely moving away from an undesired past.*

A huge part of this journey is learning to move from natural faith (faith in things we understand) to spiritual faith (faith in things we may not understand). This is not meant to be a deeply religious book but, in it I unashamedly use principles from the Bible. They are tried, proven, ageless, and culture-transcendent. And they work!

These principles are not isolated to minority or Christian groups nor are they governed by human performance and achievement. They don't favor a particular gender, race, socioeconomic position, or religion. They are so simple that even the most simple among us can experience a radical transformation in life!

I'm sure from your own story, you will agree with me that life is never perfect and that it is often unfair. Perhaps, like me, you have cried out, "Take me back to when it was all okay, right before it all went wrong!" Actually, I'm going to go one step further—I'm going to show you how to get to a place that is better than the one before it all went wrong!

The truth is that bad things do happen to good people. I think I'm a pretty good person but I have known my fair share of the bad—the stuff that should really be dished out to those deserving it! But unfortunately, as citizens of planet earth and colleagues of humanity, it comes with the territory. Some don't get the good things they deserve and some get good things they don't deserve.

Mostly, we can neither stop bad things from happening to us nor prevent them from hurting us; but we can end the cycle in which bad experiences create a lose/lose for us. We can pause, breathe, and take in a new perspective. This book will show you that it is absolutely possible to get to a place where life is okay . . . to a place where everyone is winning again.

Although life's experiences consist of winter moments of pain, barrenness, frustration, and disappointment, it also consists of exquisite times of joy, pleasure, and contentment. It is natural and healthy to want more of the good times but most of us have had times of feeling robbed or cheated of those good things in life.

Most of us know what it is like to have our journey sabotaged or roadblocked and we know what it's like to end up feeling that we have missed out on the best we had coming to us . . . that we are existing rather than really living! We suspect there is more to life but we don't know how to get it!

I was in this place—the winter season; the bad and unfair times; the times when it seemed that everyone around me was losing, including me. In that place, I discovered that I could journey into life in a forward momentum without the persistent urge to look back and set up camp in the "Why," "What's the point?" and "Why me?" questions that lead to a place called "stuck." *A Fascination with Forward* is the end result of those discoveries.

BACKWARD QUESTIONS

Without even being consciously aware of it, there are backward and forward questions you have conditioned yourself to ask.

The backward questions raise scenarios and feelings that keep us in places of hurt or regret; places that position us at the mercy of circumstances, people, words, and actions. And so, victimized by whatever wrongs have been done to us, we become disempowered by convincing ourselves that we are not in control and that we will never live the life of our dreams.

Frustration and anger become common friends of our thought life, taking up residence and draining our soul of any bright hope we once held as our right of destiny. We soon lose momentum and become roadblocked by our own rear-vision mirror. Does this sound familiar?

Such questions might be:
- Why didn't I . . . . ?
- What's the point?
- How come they are getting away with it?
- Why me?
- Is this all there is?

FORWARD QUESTIONS

Forward questions, on the other hand, are the possibility questions.

They actually create margins in our thought life which make room for reigniting hopes and dreams.

These questions create forward momentum by opening our minds to move beyond the past and even out of the present. We are no longer at the mercy of circumstances, people, words, or actions but are right into, and back into, the liberating realm of our potential and our dreams! They are the "How do I make me better?" questions. They are the questions that can lead us out of Stuckville, giving us back the control of our lives, assuring us that we are still living in Plan A.

Such questions might be:

- Why not?
- What's possible?
- How will I?
- How do I want this to look?
- What outcome do I want from this?
- What does this say about me?
- Are there other perspectives?
- Am I missing something?

Principle—Forward questions help me create margins in my thought life for fresh momentum through positive possibility pictures.

- I am going to be honest about the progress I have made in my life.
- I am going to set out some achievable goals for my life if I have not already done so.
- I identify the paralyzing backward questions that keep me stuck.
- I replace them with forward questions that will inspire me and awaken or reawaken my dreams.
- I dare ask myself, "Is it possible that this year could be my best yet?"

My hope is that you will be moved by this principle rather than enslaved by your circumstances; that you will live in the realm of your dreams; and that you will take others with you.

— CHAPTER ONE —

CHECKING OUT OF STUCKVILLE

— CHAPTER ONE —

CHECKING OUT OF STUCKVILLE

For me, one of the most frustrating things in life is being stuck in traffic! I never have "all day" when I'm stuck in traffic. Even when I don't have any pressing deadlines, being stuck in traffic suddenly creates some! I get a surge of claustrophobic urgency to get out of there and an impatient frustration builds when I can see no way around the delay! Breathe!

The M1, the main highway leading from the Gold Coast to Brisbane, has in recent years been expanded to cope with the increased migration to our (some say "perfect") Australian Sunshine State. However, there are still days and predictable times and spots where the traffic congestion can bring hundreds of vehicles to a snail-paced crawl or a stand still.

Funny, isn't it? We can get so angry at unavoidable delays that we have little or no control over, and yet we often live with avoidable delays and roadblocks . . . the ones that we do have control over.

Life is supposed to be a wonderful journey that we can enjoy and share with others; living in the harmony and collaboration of community; creating memories and digging wells of experience that can be drawn from at various points to help nurture our own life and assist those around us. But often we find the wells empty, the roads blocked, and the memories sour.

We have been created to thrive in an environment with all we need to fill our wells and to keep us resourced for the future. But when we live in the realm of backward questions—"Why did this have to happen?"; "Why should I?"; "What's the point?" (questions that fuel anger and stir up hurt and resentment)—we delay our progress, roadblock our path and drain our well.

How does this happen? The harmony, relationships, and collaboration with community, family, friends, or others in our world (the very people who help fill our well) cease or are diminished because life becomes about "me" and the impact they have had on "me." Everyone in our world seems to end up losing, including "me."

A PLACE CALLED STUCKVILLE

On the motorway during slow moving traffic or with any sniff of a hold up, the first thing I look for is an exit route. I want out of there! I want to avoid a potential collision or lengthy delay and I'll take the nearest exit even if it's going to take me the long way to my destination. Why? Probably because I'm impatient, but also because I'm thinking forward. I'm thinking of where I am going; why it's important for me to get there; when I want to arrive; what I'll do when I get there; and how that's where I want to be! I guess I have a fascination with forward.

But sometimes, there are unavoidable delays in our journey that either take us by surprise or gradually wound us taking us to a place called Stuckville.

It is a valley with many roads leading in but few leading out. It is a place that accommodates those whose dreams have been nailed to the crucible of another's actions; those whose hopes have been dashed by random circumstances; those whose identity has been raped at the hand of someone unsure of their own.

Some just wander into Stuckville exhausted from trying and resigned to existing. Some wind up there as a result of decisions others made. Some inadvertently sabotage their own lives through fear of their own brilliance or ignorant of their own potential and Stuckville becomes their home away from home.

The exit signs out of Stuckville are clearly sign-posted but we don't easily see them, mostly because we are still wondering how we landed in Stuckville in the first place.

We can either blame ourselves or someone else but, once there, we easily begin thinking that this must be our lot . . . that it must be what we deserved for not being enterprising enough, loving enough, good enough, or smart enough (thoughts that spring up so readily from empty wells.)

When I arrived there, it wasn't by my deliberate choice (it never is) and I found myself wondering where I had gone wrong. The thought of setting up house there and adapting to Stuckville's culture—financially, relationally, socially, and spiritually—was so misaligned with all the vision and dreams I had incubating inside me that I became physically sick and spiritually confused.

The Road In

I arrived at Stuckville after my husband of almost seventeen years and father of our two sons left our family. I soon recognized the valley—you probably know it too. It has smooth and welcoming entries that appear just after we hit the roadblock. Remember? We never get there kicking and screaming. Such freedom fights are for those who have steely convictions about their true core values and the worth of their own dreams. No, it's all downhill to Stuckville and we glide in unintentionally steered by our emotions and circumstances and fueled by our backward questions.

I was not a complete novice in the matter of sorrow having helped others through their pain. Yet I was so consumed by my own backward questions and by hanging onto my little family by a thread that I now desperately needed to find my own road out—an exit route to a better future.

Feeling sorry for ourselves for too long is paralyzing and putting up with ourselves in that state for too long is debilitating. All too soon we get so used to our own self-imposed restrictions and limitations that we discover Plan B is not the second chance we hoped for but merely second best.

The Road Out

The road called "forgiveness" became my exit route. Its power fueled my determination to get out and move forward; its extraordinary methods empowered my capacity to live an extraordinary life! And it can definitely be your exit route, too.

This route takes energy, determination, and resources we think we don't have and that thinking makes us double-minded and unconvinced of the result-for-effort.

It's like being offered an escape or exit route away from an oncoming bushfire that will consume us. But we choose to stay put—wait it out, fight it out, reason it out, work it out, suffer it out. And before we know it, we get burnt!

Stuckville's lame culture is founded on the old adage of "better the devil we know than the one we don't." Actually, it's more than an adage; it's a lie that is easy to believe. We probably don't like where we are but we also don't like the thought of risking a new path either. We're exhausted, sick of the fight, and disillusioned by the results. We want an exit or detour route that not only gets us out of the jam and back on the road to our dreams but we want it to be the quickest way out with the least amount of sacrifice or effort!

However, winning a few fights doesn't mean winning the battle. Immediate gratification doesn't guarantee long-term contentment. Unfortunately, most people think that, considering all they have been through, they deserve easy street; or, considering all they have been through, that they don't have the energy to invest into tomorrow or the vision to see beyond today. Hello Stuckville! If this is describing your situation, if your responses keep getting you the same common results, then it's time to try something uncommon!

> *Making decisions to create the now we desire will only bring temporary solutions and short-term contentment; but making decisions to create the future we desire will bring lasting and fulfilling contentment.*

Choosing a road that leads us upward, onward, and forward to the future that we are designed, purposed, and resourced for—a road with our name on it—is worth exploring!

However, I must warn you—the journey forward will require you to pay attention to new sign posts. You will have to stop listening to your old internal satellite navigation system (the familiar voices that used to direct you—voices from your past that have the power to take you back and voices around you that have the power to keep you in the present) and begin listening to new voices that will take you safely and surely toward your destiny.

- The road may be narrow. That's okay. Lean into the people around you who are on this journey also.
- The route may be uncharted. That's okay. Be fueled by forward questions; read the sign posts; trust your decisions.
- And oh yes, you may need to leave some luggage behind. That's okay, too, because it will make room for new supplies and resources that you will pick up along the way. (We'll talk more about that later.)

FACING THE 'F' WORD

C.S Lewis wrote in his book *Mere Christianity*: "Everyone thinks forgiveness is a lovely idea until they have something to forgive . . ."[1]

He was absolutely right. We can believe something in theory but struggle with it in practice. Why? Because mentally agreeing to something doesn't cost us anything whereas implementing something we believe in often requires us to put our life on the line, reputation out in front, name on the document, or action to the plan. That's called commitment!

Maybe it is easier to forgive a stranger—I don't know. But I do know that to forgive someone we have loved, trusted, and given our life to is quite a unique and personal matter. Someone who has known our heart but acted callously anyway, known our thoughts but denied them anyway, known our intentions but chosen carelessly anyway, known our commitment but moved away anyway, known our dreams but squashed them anyway . . . that someone is hard to forgive. Suddenly there's a whole new meaning to the *F* word!

As I found out, mentally agreeing that it is a lovely idea to forgive holds no power to move beyond the crises and no power to free us. Forgiveness must be actioned.

Forgiveness at the point of my roadblock was not even a lovely idea. I found myself alone—not lonely, but alone. I had some good friends and a healthy support network but now I was alone in my decision making, path clearing, and future creating. I was alone in my thoughts and I began hating myself and hating my life. Self blame in any crisis is quite common.

Contrary to what you may be feeling right now, you do have everything you need at your disposal to live an unchained, unplugged, unblocked, unstuck, and unusual life! But it all finds its roots in a life underscored by forgiveness.

I know this book will give you new insight into the power of forgiveness—how it can free, heal, and uncomplicate you. My hope is that you will choose this path for yourself. I invite you to let my journey fast forward yours. Fight the giants—for yourself, for your family, for a generation you may never meet.

> *You may not have control over everything but you have control over some things. You can change the world by changing your world.*

Allow me to guide you to signposts out of Stuckville and through the times when you may be unconvinced of results-for-effort; times when forgiveness does not seem to be a lovely idea.

Principle—I will focus on what I can control.
- Rather than getting angry at the unavoidable delays in my journey over which I have little or no control, I refuse to live with avoidable delays and roadblocks over which I do have control.
- I choose to have a hunger for something better and to make decisions that will create the future I desire.
- I choose to listen to some new voices that will draw me out of the past, beyond the present, and into my future.

CHAPTER TWO

THE FRIGHTENING THOUGHT OF LIVING IN PLAN B

(OR . . . DON'T GIVE UP ON PLAN A!)

THE FRIGHTENING THOUGHT OF LIVING IN PLAN B

(OR . . . DON'T GIVE UP ON PLAN A!)

After any crisis or profound life-altering event, our emotions will begin to convince our mind that it is going to be plan B from now on; that plan A is over; and that we can never go back and reclaim the lost ground. Perhaps these places of pain or regret show us a picture of a lost partner or friend; perhaps a dissolved marriage, a failed business, a wrong choice, a bad decision or lost opportunities.

Perhaps our own private pain produces internal pictures that no one else will ever see or quite understand. And so we resign ourselves to thinking that life will always look a certain way from now on and that second best is the most we can ever look forward to.

Subconsciously we may think, "I can never forget because I will always carry these scars and these scars separate me from everyone else." There are times when these subconscious thoughts become an escape and an excuse to shy away, hide, or retreat from fully engaging in life and relationships.

Sometimes, they may make us so self conscious that we believe we are wearing some sort of sign on our forehead signaling our "condition"—"Recently Divorced," "Newly separated," "Wrongly Accused," "Cruelly Abandoned," "Sexually Abused," "Business Failure," "Embarrassingly Rejected,"

"Verbally Berated," "Recently Demoted," "Unemployed," "Single parent." Even if it's mostly in our imagination, it's real for us which means that we still have to deal with it.

If you are identifying with this, I have to say this to you . . .

We may not be able to change the look of our start but we can change the look of our ending. We may not be able to have a second chance but we can make a fresh beginning.

Throughout the book, as I share some of my own journey, the inconvenient detours and unseen roadblocks, and by asking forward questions, especially those that are seldom asked, you will be given space to internalize and personalize the principles and lessons learned. It's important to take the time to think them through and to be honest with yourself as you uncover truth and mine the wisdom necessary to become the person you desire to be.

I encourage you to read this with a pen in hand to underline, thoughtfully ponder and answer the posed questions, jotting down your own thoughts.

A new friend who has since become a good friend once whispered into my ear as she carefully and empathetically hugged me, "You know, I don't have to understand your pain to understand pain." And she was right. She didn't fully understand my pain but she had known intense pain and excruciating disappointment in her own life. It was enough.

We will never know the personal pain of another but ours will bring a connection with them that holds the keys to their journey back to life and to their Plan A. I do not pretend to know your pain but because pain is so universal and healing is less, so I feel compelled to share how the most exhilarating revelations can emerge from the deepest places of debilitation.

When my first husband left, I found myself not only emotionally wounded but in a head spin—literally! This didn't happen to our family and so it couldn't possibly be happening to me! Don't say the *D* word because we don't have divorce in our family! I thought I had been a good wife and mother. I may not have done everything right but I'd done everything I knew to do. I thought we had been good friends and committed partners. I thought.

What do we do with the picture of our future when it is now clearly never going to happen? My promise and values looked like "through thick and thin till death do us part." Surely there was nothing that couldn't be worked through! Whatever the circumstances, I thought we could come back to the negotiating table and draw up new terms and conditions—work it out —renew our vows and love—begin afresh! But over the next few months I realized this was clearly never going to happen. I felt like my life just ceased. Plan B loomed in the background and I began to believe its voice of second best.

THE VALUE FACTOR . . . SPECIFICALLY . . . WE ARE STILL VALUABLE!

The tragic fallout of crises is seen in the effect it has on the human psyche. Second best becomes the philosophy and Plan B doesn't have to be devised; it just evolves itself through self-sabotaging thoughts.

Death, abandonment, rejection, catastrophe, abuse, violation can all leave a person feeling diminished in value. Somehow, just by association, a person will feel responsible for the attraction of the crisis. "Why did this happen to me?"; "Am I less important than her?"; "Am I less spiritual than him?" "This sort of thing would never happen to them!"

Sometimes there is even a subconscious acceptance that we have deserved it.

The degree to which people accept lingering blame, hurt, and a Plan B mentality is directly proportional to the degree of value they believe about themselves.

A lack of personal value undermines all attempts of outside help and assistance. Whatever is offered will be seen as charity rather than a step toward empowerment. Have you ever caught yourself saying, "Oh, well, I guess I'll just have to live with it"; or "I'll just have to make the most of what I've got"; or "I can't see things ever changing." These are the statements of diminished value.

We will only ever live the life we think we deserve.

The rise of the motivational speakers and seminars in the last twenty years or so has placed a new focus on self-worth. The words "self-esteem" have become vogue and people are being taught to think positively, believe bigger, expect better, and visualize their picture-perfect future. On the whole, people have been moved, changed, and healed. These principles are good. The methods of motivating and energizing people through recognizing *key inner drivers* are good and almost draw a parallel with the principles of the Bible. With or without a dynamic Christian faith, one can apply these principles and they will work.

However, outstanding and sustained outcomes can be experienced from living a lifestyle that includes God. Instead of going it alone, we find ourselves in a unique partnership where he brings what we need to the table. The power lies in this knowledge:

- that, when we have nothing left, he still has
- that, when we feel powerless or weak, he is our strength
- that, when we have exhausted all our resources, he still has some
- that, when we don't know what to do next, he will show us
- that, when we feel inadequate or worthless, he restores our dignity and confirms our value.

So our key inner drivers are fueled not merely from *positive thinking but from higher thinking*. We become driven not merely by what we think but by what God thinks. Our value then doesn't fluctuate with the circumstances and isn't reliant on an exercise in mustering up internal motivation. Rather, it's a belief that God believes in us despite the circumstances! Surprisingly, this magnificent discovery shines the brightest when we need it the most—when we are at the end of ourselves.

The thing I love most about value that is derived from a relationship and significance in God is this—the more we acknowledge our own value, the more we see the value in others. People in our world are liberated, promoted, and esteemed simply because we gave ourselves that gift first. Recognized value gives us and the people in our world permission to shine and thrive. But where does it come from and how do we regain it when it is lost?

When we acknowledge God in our life, we become elevated above our own thoughts of origin and destiny to a realm governed by love, purpose, and higher meaning. We cease being (at best) developed or evolved animals or (at worst) rearranged space matter . . . and become created beings wearing the fingerprint of God and thereby sealed with infinite value.

God reveals his heart and character through the ancient writers. Isaiah was one such writer who affirmed that God is our creator and that we are in his care even before we are born.[2]

For Christmas one year, my two sons each received a cricket bat—smaller in size than a certified bat and cheaper in quality. What made the bats so special were the signatures they bore. They were limited edition collectors' bats signed by the Australian heroes of the cricket world. These bats became more valuable than any test match bat. It wasn't the bat but the signatures they bore that made the difference.

What makes us so special is not our body, nor qualifications, nor impressive line-up of achievements but the fact that we are God's workmanship, his work of art bearing his signature. We are significant not because of what we do but because of whose we are—children of God.

John was another ancient writer and close friend of Jesus. He wrote excitedly, like he'd just discovered it for himself about how amazing it was to be loved so much that we would be called God's children.[3] Then he repeats it again.

I love that emphasized repeat—"We really are his children." It's like John knew that most of us would shake our heads in disbelief and say, "No. Not me. Billy Graham maybe, Mother Theresa maybe, Martin Luther King maybe, but not me." If that's what we think then John added that line for us. "We really are his children." And as his children, what's important to us is important to him because we are valued.

If we can find our lasting value in God, we are more likely to accept forgiveness for ourselves and thus be able to offer it to another. Our lives then become marked by peace and our world becomes underscored by community. We suddenly become worth forgiving and others become worth the effort.

We are less likely to be governed long term by circumstances, incidents, accidents, intrusive behavior from others, mistakes, and manipulative voices. Why? Because we believe life holds purpose; that our thoughts and opinions matter; that our feelings are valid; and that our dreams are real and within reach.

At this point in my own journey,

*I reinforced myself with reminders of value.
I began to outgrow the comparisons I had made
against the "perfect" lives around me. I outgrew the
victim mindset of Plan B. Lastly, I outgrew the
guilt of being associated with the crisis.*

Principle—I am significant . . . not because of what I do but because of whose I am.

- I recognize that I may have (even unintentionally) resigned myself to living Plan B.
- I am aware of the self-sabotaging thoughts that led me to that place.
- I realize that my view of the future is affected by realizing that I am valued by God and by claiming a new sense of personal value.

CHAPTER THREE

WHEN DREAMS FALL INTO A COMA

WHEN DREAMS FALL INTO A COMA

I attended university after school gaining a degree and career in children's dentistry with health education and promotion being my greatest strength. This was my life from school until I had my children. Little did I know that I would soon move back into dentistry to put food on the table and pay the bills for our now downsized family of three.

My dream, however, was far from clinics and health forums. As a fourth generation Christian, I was raised in a family that not only believed in God's timeless principles but was an amazing example of how life looked when people actually lived according to what they believed. My dad didn't so much practice what he preached; rather, he preached what he practiced. His example made this extraordinary life real, within reach, and achievable—and it impacted me forever.

I always dreamed of trading clinic for lectern and not just the lecterns in churches. I also saw myself in school halls, behind corporate lecterns, and in community seminars (all of which are a regular part of my life now!). I had a passion to teach and speak. I knew these ancient yet contemporary Biblical keys worked in my own life and equally knew they would work for others. I was compelled.

When I was twelve years old, I had the dream for the first time. I stood on the kiosk steps of the camping ground where my parents took us each year in the summer holidays. At the foot of the Grampian Mountains and set on a beautiful lake, the area attracted people from all over our home state of Victoria. They were attracted to swimming, climbing, bush walking, fishing, and sailing. In my dream, they were attracted to me.

I stood tall and spoke eloquently and boldly and they listened. They asked questions and I had the answers—every one. When I awoke from the dream, I had a profound sense of the accurate and passionate content of my delivery but I could not remember exactly what I had spoken nor could I relate to the confident and capable "me" in the dream. But I had a secret desire to be her.

I went on to dream that same dream at two other random times throughout my life. I knew that one day the time would be right but the assignments of university, marriage (that had become all consuming in its difficulties), career, and children all needed my attention and priority.

And then the unthinkable—he left. The timing of such things is never planned and so cannot be planned for.

With the heartbreaking realization of abandonment and of having to enter the next season as a single parent, I briefly lost sight of my passion and many of my dreams. (That statement is an obvious truth but also a resounding understatement!) My world fell apart! The compelling voices of dreams and visions became faint and mostly drowned out by my own sense of failure and the harsh reality of bills, fees, pressures, and the natural instinct for survival—both physical and emotional.

Anyway, would the church still accept me in a leadership position—me, now a *single mother*? More to the point, would the church accept me in a leadership position—me, now as a *divorced woman*? I decided that the answer to both questions was "no" and thus I became acutely aware that I had just become another statistic! We should be careful how we define ourselves!

What we allow to define us could confine us!

The ignorant picture I had of single mothers painted a picture of me driving an old car, having an unkept garden and unruly kids! I saw myself as queen of the preloved, the secondhand, the borrowed, and living from month to month. The thought of it diminished me and kept me small.

Then I saw her!

There is a short story in the Bible which snuck its way into another story in the New Testament book of Mark, chapter 5, beginning at verse 21.[4] It is the story of an audacious act by a desperate woman. She mustered up the courage (against cultural stigmas of the time) to push her way through crowds of people to Jesus who was on his way to the home of a city official. This woman was sick, really sick. She had a bleeding disorder that culturally branded her "unclean" and demanded her isolation. Over many years, she had spent all her money on remedies and doctors to no avail, and now here she was. Jesus was on his way to other more pressing needs when she touched his coat with a last audacious effort of faith believing that he would heal her. And he did!

Such faith attracts the attention and draws the compassionate heart of God right into any situation. She defined herself as a sick woman and so was confined by her condition—until she stepped out in faith. She was both defined and confined by the social stigma of "unclean" and so was relegated to living out a Plan B existence. Was this surge of belief brought about by a brief glimpse at a Plan A possibility? With her, healing would now come a redefinition and a bright future socially, culturally, and physically. It's funny how those who are familiar with the story still refer to it as "the woman with the issue of blood." This may have been the beginning of her story but it was not the end.

We need to be careful how we define ourselves and how we allow others to define us. Definitions influence the way we think and determine the level of life we are willing to accept.

After seeing her, I saw him!

Blind Bartimeus slipped in at the end of that same New Testament book of Mark in chapter 10.[5] He didn't die blind! He received full sight and social elevation. Here is his story. Here he was sitting by the road begging—a professional beggar licensed to wear the traditional beggar's cloak. When Jesus came near, he cried out the typical confession of a beggar, "Jesus, Son of David, have mercy on me!" But this time, there was something in his heart and attitude that caught the compassionate attention of Jesus.

We don't even know his name. "Bar" means "son of" and so this blind beggar was the son of some man called Time-us. Just some blind guy.

When he heard that Jesus was approaching him, he did something extraordinary. He stood up and took off his beggar's cloak. He removed what defined him even before he received what he was hoping for! Jesus then asked him an obvious question, "What do you want me to do for you?" He answered, "Great One, I want to see." In doing this, even before he received his sight, Jesus required him to identify his need, to look forward and to redefine himself as a whole and healed person.

Having seen these two remarkable Bible characters, I turned my attention back to my situation. Who would take me seriously? I was so self-conscious of my newly unwanted title that I thought people could actually see me coming. I wasn't wearing a blind beggar's cloak nor did I carry the "unclean" sign of the menstruating woman; but *D* for divorce was painted on my forehead. Maybe they would think that I was "one of those poor women," or worse, "one of those women wanting the freedom from the constraints of marriage." Real or imagined, it became my roadblock and my worst enemy. It had the potential to both define me and confine me.

During the wretchedness of that first year of single mummy-ing, I resigned myself to a long life in Plan B. Plan A (being happily married and raising our family in the love and security of our marriage unit) hadn't worked out—and I was so sorry to God that it hadn't. On the good days, I was sorry that my life now looked like this but on my worst days I would yell at God demanding to know why and where he was in all this! Had he not seen my efforts, heard my prayers, understood my struggles, and known my heart? Punish the ones that deserve it but don't punish me!

My backward questions like, "Why did this happen to me?"; "How can I live with this?"; "Where were you all this time God?" led me slowly to Stuckville . . . no conceivable way out, no possible way to get ahead. I would often wonder: "Was God okay with all that had transpired?"; "Had I missed out on his best for me?"; "Had I messed up his plan which would affect my life forever?" I would also wonder about the effect my life's path would have on my boys. I wondered if God, like me, was taken by surprise . . . a holy "bother, didn't see that coming so what do I do with Deborah now?"

Then I would recall the stories of Bartimeus, the woman, and others like them. For them, there was no conceivable way out until they believed in someone greater and in something better.

Principle—What I allow to define me could confine me.

- I take responsibility for questions and concepts which have held me in Plan B living.
- I choose to reengage with forgotten dreams, visions, or plans, still accepting them as my Plan A.

— CHAPTER FOUR —

UNDERSTANDING SEASONS

UNDERSTANDING SEASONS

As I began to revisit my dreams, a new realization dawned on me. I had to learn to appreciate the season even when I hated the weather. The wise man of ancient writings penned these intriguing words:

> *The race is not to the swift, nor the battle to the strong,*
> *nor bread to the wise, nor riches of men to understanding,*
> *nor favour to men of skill;*
> *but time and chance happen to them all.*[6]

The thing about God, time, and opportunities is this: they are available to us all and not (as we often think) limited to the privileged, the lucky or those better than ourselves. We have constructed an organized schedule that facilitates human life between sunrise and sunset; between January and December; between summer and spring; between calendar years, school terms, and financial years and nine to five; between preschool, adolescence, teens, adult, midlife, and senior years; between childbearing years, peak career, and retirement years. We set our goals, expectations, and plans around these time frames. We become obsessed with time management and disappointed with lost or wasted time.

But time cannot be managed . . . only people's actions.
Time cannot be lost or wasted . . . only people's opportunities.

Before any time frames existed, there was God. He created the days and the seasons and us. His words recorded in the first book of the Bible called Genesis reveal that his best plan for humanity included seasons.[7] What we learn about natural seasons helps us to understand spiritual seasons.

Too many people endure too much, suffer too long, and live too narrowly because they do not understand the nature of seasons.

There are three main things to know about seasons. When they are understood, they help us navigate through life with wisdom.

1. SEASONS ARE GOD-ORDAINED

Right from the beginning, God created seasons as his very best plan for life on planet earth. In the first book of the Bible called Genesis, the phrase "God said" occurs about ten times as he creatively speaks and brings about life and order.[8] (I can remember discussing this with my family around our parent's kitchen table when my little five-year-old nephew interrupted with, "I don't see why God had to rest on the seventh day. All he did was talk!") Good point! . . . until we understand the authority and power in God's words.

He first separates and breaks up the darkness by his word which causes an explosion of light. (How many times have we longed for an explosion of light to break in on our darkness?) An interesting side fact is the original Hebrew meaning of the words:

light = order and structure
darkness = chaos and unformed or void

So in creating the first season of twenty-four hours called a day, God breaks in on the chaos of darkness to inject light, structure, order, and symmetry.

A few chapters later, he reinforces his creative purpose by declaring:

"While the earth remains, seed time and harvest, cold and heat, winter and summer and day and night shall not cease." Genesis 8: 22 (New King James Version)

Principle—God created seasons as his best plan for life on planet Earth.

- Within my current season, I choose to live in light (order, sense, structure, purpose, and divine intelligence) rather than darkness (chaos, mess, disappointment, and sadness.)
- I am going to actively ponder and plan how that could and should look.
- Because my words carry power, I take responsibility for how I speak of my circumstances so those words reconnect with my dreams.

2. SEASONS ARE TEMPORARY

Seasons are never meant to be eternal or perpetual. In the same book of Genesis, there is a little five-word phrase repeated about forty-nine times that helps tell the story of how people transition their life's events from one season to another. The phrase is, "And it came to pass . . ." This tells us that it doesn't come to stay! Whatever the situation, it ends . . . and the people concerned move into a new season. They move on. Things changed.

For me, one such seasonal change came unexpectedly. After a seven-year season of being a single mum, a new season arrived and took my breath away! I met Philip Candler and so together we became a "Mr. and Mrs." again.

I once caught myself watching a young mum nursing a new born from across a crowded room. Phil and I were attending a work function for a firm where her husband held an upper management position and so she had made the effort to attend. She chose her position in a quiet corner more, I suspect, for her benefit than the baby's and was periodically pulling at her dress and smoothing her hair.

I recognized it at once. Nothing fitted. Her dark, glazed eyes were a dead giveaway—she was seriously sleep deprived, stressed, and self-conscious. I made my way over. New babies are an easy conversation starter. I whispered into her ear, "We are not bad mums if we occasionally feel like leaving our baby by the side of the road." We both giggled. Then, as if I had been reading her mind, her eyes filled with tears. Tears come easily when we're tired. I encouraged her that fatigue wears us all down and that, no matter how difficult this season was, it too would pass.

We can so easily become consumed by the details of the present. Tunnel vision will cause us to see only the products of the season we are in. Preparing our mind for the next season is vital (even if the one we are in is killing us) because this present one will not last forever.

This is great news if we are roadblocked or stuck in a season of disappointment, regret, hurt, anger, loss or drought. Morning will come; spring will come; daylight will come. How do I know? Because it always does! Each season is designed with the DNA to move forward and so are we. But we hold the keys that determine when that will be and how that will look.

In some cultures where there has been the loss of a spouse, the remaining grieving partner will wear black for the remainder of their life—long after that season has gone. Every day the person will wear the clothes that belong to another season. Every day they restrict themselves from moving forward because their outward behavior is a constant reminder of a season that is long past. This cultural habit creates a perpetual season of grieving and sad memories.

Seasons are temporary. This is not to diminish a great season or dampen one that's fun and working for us. Each season is designed to be built upon; improved with wisdom, hindsight, knowledge, and life lessons. Even in the best seasons of our life, we can be drawing out knowledge, refining our skills, storing away wisdom, and nurturing relationships that will benefit us in the future.

Principle—Each season carries within it the DNA to move forward.

- The only person who can keep me from entering another season is me.

- I will now identify memories, heartache, unforgiveness, regret, or bitterness that has caused me to create a perpetual season and so keep me from moving into another season.

- Likewise, I take responsibility for things I have let go prematurely, hung on to for too long, thrown away hastily, picked up unwisely, or dragged out for too long.

- Mindful of these things, I now embrace positive thoughts and actions that will prepare my mind for my next season.

3.   SEASONS ARE SEQUENTIAL

This is perhaps the most important factor to remember about seasons. Each one is dependent upon the other. Each is linked to the one that preceded it and to the one that will follow it. Every time God said, "Let there be . . . ," His words manifested something that would draw its life from what came before and give life and purpose to what would come next.

No season exists for its own purpose but for the function of ushering in a new season and to produce a harvest. And we all want to see the fruit! Each season holds the DNA for the next season. Or we could say that each season is pregnant with the seeds of the next season.

The season we are in today (regardless of the weather) holds vital information, lessons, connections, and opportunities that will assist us to transition into the next season and help us control the weather! What we do in this season will impact the next season because they are linked and sequential.

Principle—Each season is linked to the one that preceded it and to the one that will follow it.

- Not everything in my current season has come from God and not everything in this season was God's intended best for me but I am the only person who can diminish the potential and intended purpose of this season.
- I identify patterns in my behavior, decision making, and thinking that impact my life.
- Lessons from this season will assist me to create better patterns for my future.

The season of winter will often cause us to hibernate indoors. We want to stay dry and warm while we dream of spring and hope for summer. Deciduous trees lose their leaves and look stark against a gray sky and void of any sign of life.

While I was growing up, we had a variety of fruit trees growing in our back yard. Each year we enjoyed nectarines, plums, apricots, peaches, grapes, and apples. If we had lopped them off because they looked dead in winter, our actions would have denied us the pleasure they brought us in summer.

During autumn when their spent leaves fell to the ground and in winter when their naked branches looked stark and lifeless against a gray winter backdrop, something was going on inside the DNA of our trees that was vitally important to their next fruit-bearing season. We couldn't see it, we didn't benefit from it and yet . . .

Dad fertilized the soil, weeded the root base and removed excess branches. Why? Because he did what was needed when there was no fruit so he would get what he wanted when it was the season for fruit.

With first-hand evidence from the orchards of my childhood, I can assure you that you *will* enter another season and that the one you are in is temporary and sequential . . . not permanent. Autumn will follow summer and winter will follow autumn and spring will follow winter and summer will shine its warmth again before you know it! Because it always does!

It's not so much about recognizing the season or moving into another season as it is about knowing what to do and applying the right behaviors in each season.

God's "It came to pass" indicated that one season had ended and another was about to begin. This is good news if winter has us believing that our world is stark against a cold backdrop. It's great news if we are about to lop off our dreams thinking that they had died with the season. What we believe about this season—what we say about it, decide to do in it and how we behave through it—is building the DNA for the next season and will determine the fruit we produce.

> *Don't be deceived into thinking that whoever or whatever has gone, left or been taken from our life automatically ushers in Plan B.*

A good horticulturist knows there is a season to prune and that pruning will encourage new growth. Although pruning has an "ouch" sound to it, those snippers can actually do us a lot of favors! Jesus explained this to a group of friends one day reminding them that pruning is a healthy and necessary component of growth.[9] His friends knew him well enough to know that the plant illustrations were not an encouragement to develop their gardening skills but that they had a deeper and more significant meaning for them as men, women, and as leaders.

Pruning will remove old, dead, or unproductive branches, reducing the amount of energy the plant has to put into sustaining them. Pruning will remove top-heavy branches that cause the plant to bend under the weight. Pruning ignites the plant's growth spurt encouraging new leafy shoots to spring forth. Whatever has been taken from us or whoever has left, don't despair. In fact, take hope—we probably won't need them in the next season we are moving into!

> ### Principle—If I do what is needed when there is no fruit, I will get what I want when the season for fruit arrives.
>
> * I recognize places in my life into which I have been pouring energy without any resulting productivity.
> * I am equally aware of unwanted weights (top-heaviness) that are causing me to bend.
> * If I am to prune, I will do so carefully, thoughtfully, and with wisdom.
> * Equally, I will be careful not to prune, but rather to fertilize, things I have stopped doing because it is "not the season" . . . things that, if I continue to nurture them, could reward me in the future.

These lessons from our little backyard garden were generally true and paint a quaint metaphor for life's journey. However, it is equally true to recognize that the seasons of nature are occasionally intercepted by freak or uncommon patterns, just like our lives. Throughout history and across the earth, people have experienced the devastating effects of drought, earthquakes, floods, and famine. The question "What must I do in this season?" remains. The question "Who will I be when this season ends?" also remains.

Often when unseasonable pain strikes, it becomes our reference point from then on. There was life before the pain and there is life after the pain. Before, we could see life and even God clearly. After the pain, the future doesn't seem so clear and God does not seem so near. Pain can distort the view but it cannot block it, eclipse it or snuff it out—just distort it. When our view has been distorted by unseasonable weather, we may need to reposition ourselves a little to be able to see again.

Let me tell you about a penny dropping revelation that hit me in a quiet moment this side of winter. I was reading an ancient letter from the once "anti-everything Christian, turned believer"— Paul. In the book of Ephesians chapter 5 and verse 15, he is urging his readers not to live foolishly but wisely, redeeming the time. Then it struck me. We can redeem time! That's not to say we will relive the past but rather, we can relive the future. Do you see it? We can live out a new version of the old picture. Sure it will look and feel different but different doesn't have to be second best. It will however, be greatly shaped by what we do with God, time, and opportunities.

Birthing Dreams

During the season of pregnancy, a woman experiences the formation and growth of new life. The purpose of the nine-month season is three fold:

1.   This new life requires nine months of development to be able to adequately survive outside the nurturing environment of its mother. A diligent new mum will eat healthily, get regular check-ups and attain knowledge that will benefit her and her baby through this season.

Our next season holds opportunities that far exceed the ones from the last season. Why? Because we have acquired, learned, experienced, attained, and tasted things that have increased our capacity for life and so life expects good stewardship from our wisdom and understanding. Think of it like this—

> *Our life's journey is like digging wells along the way; each one holds the essence of what we felt, how we grew, how we grieved, how we responded and what we learned.*

Our life can literally become a torch that lights the path of another or sheds light in some one else's dark places.

Out of our wells of resource we can draw insight, perspective, experience, empathy, mercy, and wisdom. (Although it is not the purpose of this book to discuss the matter in depth, nurturing of ourselves is crucial during this time.)

2.   The second reason for the duration of pregnancy is that the mother requires nine months for her body to adjust to such an extraordinary rate of growth within her. Ligaments, muscles and bones all move and stretch to accommodate her new life form. If a baby grew to birth weight and size in a fraction of the required time, its birth would literally kill the mother and her baby would be given to another to raise.

We are designed to fulfill our dreams and know the joy of them. The seasons of life offer the invaluable gift of our character development ensuring we are bigger than the thing we are going to birth, that we are ready to raise it, and that we are safe guarding it against someone foreign taking over and adopting what was ours. Be alert to things that may need to shift, flex, grow, or change for us to be confident that we can sustain our dreams and move with positive anticipation into our next season.

3.   The third reason is so mother has time to plan and prepare. Those who confidently say "life won't change for us when we have children" have never had any! How she cares for herself—her exercise, diet, knowledge and rest—all impact on her unborn child and also on her! A few mothers will 'wing it' and fly into a baby-buying frenzy after the child is born. But for most, the nine months enables a new mum to prepare her life for a new addition.

A newly pregnant woman would be foolish to believe there is nothing going on inside her in the early weeks and months of pregnancy just because she cannot see or feel life! She would be foolish to abandon her dreams of raising a child during a period of morning sickness and tiredness because this experience and these feelings didn't match her happy mothering picture! I learned during my winter seasons that, even when it looks like nothing is happening, something is always happening!

Principle—Even when it looks like nothing is happening, something is always happening.

- My forward questions are:
- What does this season really require of me?
- What can I do differently to ensure a better outcome for the future?
- What positives can I draw from this season that will help me move forward to create a path to my dream picture of the future?
- In this season, I am digging wells of resource out of which I will draw insight, new perspectives, life lessons, experience, empathy for others, and wisdom.
- Because of the active nature of these decisions, I will discover how to nurture myself during this season.
- I realize that change is inevitable and so I will flex, shift, grow, or change in order for my dreams to be sustained in this season. Where necessary, I will change what I say and do to ensure healthy growth.

At the end of the first three months of its developing life, a fetus already has every vital organ and everything it needs to be a fully functioning adult. The remainder of time in the uterus is for the purpose of growth, maturity, and development. And yet sadly, it is during this season that babies are often aborted.

Just because we may not see any evidence of our dreams, we must be careful not to abort them because our experiences and what we are feeling don't match the picture of the future we imagined. Don't let a winter season trick you into lopping off the life you once saw because you can't see evidence of life or fruit. Additionally, don't be impatient to birth what you have inside you before the right season.

Knowing the vital nature of seasons enables us to appreciate the season even if we hate the weather right now!

— CHAPTER FIVE —

GOD CAM

GOD CAM

Have you ever driven a virtual racing car? We place our coins in the slot, put our car into gear, and select a camera angle. Our selection determines how much of the car and road ahead is in view. Each position of the car cam gives a slightly different perspective, some broader, and others more focused or narrow.

Sometimes, we may just need to change the camera angle to gain a better or clearer perspective on our life, the terrain, and the road ahead. Even the slightest shift in thinking can reveal the answers we have been searching for; reveal what was hidden to us before and cause a turnabout in our circumstances.

A new camera angle in our thinking may come about as we read books and articles about the area of our focus; it may come about as we surround our self with people who can help us see life from different levels; it may come from respected and trusted counsel, and it will definitely come from reading the Bible—God's angle.

Some of the following thoughts may be a switch of camera angle for you but stick with me and take a chance on a new perspective which may draw the curtain back on your internal windows allowing you to see a little further.

Something I have come to both know and experience is that God is neither random nor distant nor void of purpose. The good or bad circumstances of our birth are not irrelevant to a loving, purposeful, and creative father. But they are irrelevant to the seeds of capacity, potential, and resource that were placed within our DNA to ensure that we would flourish and succeed in every season of life.

Here are some poor equations that seem to be easily believed:

- MY PAST + MY BELIEFS ABOUT IT =
  MY FUTURE
- MY DNA—MY PAST = MY FUTURE

God has the advantage of seeing the beginning and the end all at once. He knows what he has so magnificently placed within us. He sees our yesterday and our today (in some measure so do we) but he also sees us from an end perspective, cheering us on. He points us to the people, resource, and opportunities in our sphere of life that will assist us over the line, out of the pit, beyond the roadblock and onto the path of our dreams. Can you recognize them? They are all around us!

The harsh realities of life that cause pain, disappointment, and regret will often cause us to see time as wasted, unproductive, and even lost. We will at the very least want to somehow make up for lost time, and, at the very worst, feel that time and chance are lost forever. But as discussed in chapter three, time cannot be wasted—only our opportunities; and it cannot be managed—only our actions.

For me, around the time of the disintegration of my first marriage, I was snagged in this sense of lost time and chance. The God Cam wasn't positioned as well as I would have expected, given my devotion to God my whole life.

I have since spent considerable time thinking about the power of heartbreak and feel that I have identified a huge and significant factor which holds us in a place of hopelessness. It is indifference.

THE TERMITE OF RELATIONSHIPS—
INDIFFERENCE

For a number of years, I experienced a numbing and restrictive pain that can be identified as one of those elusive symptoms of a troubled marriage. I now know it as the eroding pain of indifference.

Indifference looks like ordinary, feels like lukewarm and sounds like "I don't care," "I don't know," "I don't mind," "Whatever" . . .

Indifference is the cruel yet silent killer of marriages, businesses, friendships, and universal humanitarian conscience that manifests itself in coldness, conflict, misalignment, distance, and self-centeredness. Indifference says, "You don't matter enough for me to be bothered."

The root of indifference can be emotional, spiritual, physical, or geographical. If you can identify that you have been subjected to indifference or have been indifferent in a relationship that you previously held dear, it helps to identify the root of that indifference.

It is the white ant or termite of human relationships. It goes undetected because it parasites itself to other eroding problems and leaves no telltale scars. Seldom will we ever hear a person cry, "Help, I am the victim of indifference!" Yet, over time, indifference can erode and undermine even the sturdiest of foundations and the most confident personalities until there is nothing much of substance left.

For me, the pain and grief of my first husband's indifference eroded my identity and weakened my fight for survival. Then there was the divorce. This cocktail produced wounds and scars that became easy targets for my mind to recall, replay, and remember at any given time on any given day. The sting of accusation, the subtle finger of blame, the twisting stab wounds of rejection and abandonment kept my mind captive and held my body to ransom.

I would find myself asking, "Had almost seventeen years been wasted time?"; "Had my chance for happiness been lost forever?"; "Did I ever matter"; "Was anything I knew real?"

Principle—Indifference looks like ordinary, feels like lukewarm and sounds like "I don't care."

- I recognize that I have lived, or am living, with the element of indifference.
- I am able to identify the drift (emotional, spiritual, physical or geographical) which precipitated this indifference.
- I take responsibility for the insecurity and diminished sense of self-worth that is the fruit of this indifference.
- I also take responsibility for my part in the erosion and identify what was the responsibility of my significant others. If and where necessary, I will consider appropriate actions and words which will reinforce this acknowledgment.
- I rigorously separate myself from what is the responsibility of another, freeing myself from self-blame and thoughts of unworthiness (typical fruit of indifference).
- With equal rigor, I will now create a new vocabulary when speaking of myself. I will speak about who I am and who I am becoming; not what indifference caused me to be.

WHEN THE NATURAL MEETS THE SPIRITUAL

Over the course of six months, my world began to spin out of control. I ate spasmodically, lost weight, and slept for a maximum of three hours a night. In the early mornings when I would stir after just falling into a doze through sheer exhaustion, I would wake peacefully in my bed still neatly made up on his side. For a brief moment in that partially delirious state, the world was my friend and I was at peace—until reality struck me like a splash of cold water!

Adrenalin would begin to flood my veins and the morning silence would be disturbed with the sound of my own heartbeat. Reality had set in—this was now my life and I was untrained, unskilled, unprepared, and underresourced to tackle this next chapter.

Besides the confusion of ending up in a place due to decisions others made and the acute pain of a broken heart, my headspace didn't seem big enough to contain all my thoughts. Replaying scenarios became a common activity for my brain. Each time I would change a scene or two and replace them with things I wished I'd said or done—more logical comments, clever come-backs, and even more spiteful actions!

But all those exercises ever did was highlight that I was inadequate at the time; that I should have protected myself better; that the pain was still paralyzing; that it's all someone else's fault I'm living like this; and that putting two and two together over the last sixteen years just made me feel stupid and angry—with everyone!

I can remember lying on my bed one warm Sunday in March. The late afternoon sun glistened and twinkled on the pool as the breeze rippled the surface. From here, I could see across the garden I had made and the mango tree I planted for our eldest son James. That tree had special significance.

I remembered digging its hole two years earlier and planting a knee high immature mango tree at James's request. He was so excited at the prospect of lying under it on summer days and eating to his heart's delight that I couldn't resist buying another tree a few weeks later about three times its size and transplanting it into the original hole; and shifting the first tree further down the back garden. His look of unbelief when he returned from school that day showed clearly the mixture of childhood imagination and schoolboy logic. Logic won! In those few seconds, he remembered my words "water it regularly and it will grow" but he was not Jack and this was not a beanstalk. This was fun and a big tree would give fruit sooner. The tree had yielded its first fruits to us that season.

Even in my pain, I smiled as I remembered.

If I strained my position a little, I could see beyond the pool and small garden to the tennis court. Our border collie, Rolex (he is my expensive watchdog!), would corner and harass local lizards on that court, and sometimes we would find him stretched out by the net dozing in the sun with his best friend, our cat called Scan (I thought I needed a cat-scan or my head read to own a cat!).

We had held a couple of kids' birthday parties on that court. In those few seconds of memories, I smiled at the simple joys we brought into our boys' lives and the tennis matches we giggled our way through. There had been a time when I saw my marriage as James saw his mango tree . . . "Water it regularly and it will grow." But watering it didn't make it grow. I was not Cinderella and this was not my palace any more.

We had just sold the house. Actually, we hadn't made any money from the sale, just covered debt. I had one month to find rental accommodation, raise the deposit bond, and pay for removal costs. The house was no longer mine and neither was the car. Bank accounts had been closed, electricity and phone turned off. I literally had to start life again from scratch. I was this day a single mum without a single dollar.

Revenge is natural—I wanted it and you have probably wanted it too. But herein lay a problem. It was a natural response to my situation, not a spiritual response. Getting even is one of the natural laws of the jungle—dog eat dog; attack or be attacked; be a predator or become prey! But forgiveness is a law of the Kingdom of God.

Law is both a cold clinical word and a deeply emotive word. It conjures up responses of legal obligations, consequences, even fear. Yet, when the word "law" is used in the context of forgiveness/Kingdom of God, it loses its chill and is instead laden with grace. This law of forgiveness becomes a liberty . . . it is a principle gifted to us to take us beyond the natural cycle of action/revenge and into the spiritual or God way of action/forgiveness.

The Bible picture is this . . . when we receive Jesus as God's Son (Savior, restorer of our damaged soul, healer of our broken heart), we transfer our citizenship from a dark kingdom where the laws of the jungle reign, where we live independently from God; to a light kingdom where God's laws reign, where we live in eternal intimacy with God. In the light kingdom, we have access to God's heart and mind and the principle of forgiveness is a stakeholder in this process.

When the natural word meets the spiritual world, two perspectives are now before us—the things our natural eyes see and the things our spiritual eyes see. We now have our gravity and time-perspective point of view impacted by God's antigravity and timeless point of view.

What the natural eye and mind might perceive as mistakes or accidents or even tragedies, the spiritual mind and eye begins to perceive as being laced with purpose and meaning.

One of the founding fathers of the church, Apostle Paul, took the early Christians on a carefully worded journey recorded in the New Testament book of Corinthians. He told them that their natural ears and eyes will never be able to comprehend the good things of God. He then encouraged them to begin to hear and see things spiritually. He did this to introduce them to the vastness of God's infinitely creative mind compared to their finite and limited thinking. He wanted them to have a God cam. This God perspective covered not only their beginnings and endings of life but also knew the hugeness of their capacity and ability.

He then reminded them that they had access to God's ways, his heart, his character, his mind and his wisdom. Now that had to make a difference to those ancient people and it can make a difference to us today![10]

There are our ways of thinking and God's ways of thinking. Two response options now confront us—following the old patterns and seeing the old results or being open to new options to see new results.

The best way to really know God's angle on life is through reading his Word, the Bible; through honest conversational prayer and through positioning ourselves among healthy Christians who are doing life well.

But beware! Access to God's perspective on truth, life, and purpose often throw a spanner in the works of our "normal"! Even when higher perspectives or options are revealed to us, we can be reluctant to deviate far from our emotional instincts and familiar ways of thinking—for this is where we feel comfortable; this is where we feel in control; this is what comes naturally.

ANTIGRAVITY THINKING

Humanly, we have a natural inclination to think, "What goes up must come down." Isaac Newton's Law of Gravity has been wrongly applied to the spiritual, relational, financial, and emotional ebb and flow of life. With this mind set, we will more naturally ground ourselves when there's "bad weather" instead of breaking free from that limited thinking and beginning to soar.

Have you caught yourself saying, "I'm just waiting for it all to come crashing down around me,"; or "I've got the weight of the world on my shoulders,"; or "I'm feeling down today." Gravity thinking keeps us anchored to the circumstances of life.

At first, these new God perspectives may look foreign to us and we will be unconvinced of the potential freedom, health, and prosperity they hold for our life. Gravity thinking pulls us naturally toward earth.

To live above our circumstances requires thrust fuelled by trust, risk and practice—the disciplines of anti-gravity thinking.

CONDITIONED THINKING

At the time of writing, Philip and I are often in Thailand because of our work with an aid organization. On one trip, I had an interesting conversation with an elephant trainer. I asked a question about the chains that connected the front and back legs of young elephants, restricting their stride and limiting their pace. I noted that the older elephants weren't wearing these chains. His answer intrigued me.

The chain was designed to restrict the elephants' free will. If the young elephants decided to walk faster than their trainers, or run off into the crowd, small spikes would irritate their legs, making them slow down, and walk at the required pace. Over the years, they would become used to their trainers' ways, voice, and expectations until a time would come when they would be released from the chain. Now with the chain removed, these elephants would continue to walk as though the chains were still there, so strong was the conditioning. Although the elephants had their freedom, they continued to live as though they had none.

Interestingly enough, we are very similar. When confronted with new paths, new perspectives, or new ways of responding to life that can potentially free us, we will often choose to remain chained to old habits, WALKING at the same pace, not daring to take the risk, and deviate from the old conditioning.

Is it time for you to adjust your God cam?

Principle—To live higher and defy our natural inclinations requires thrust fuelled by trust, risk and disciplines of antigravity thinking.

- In which areas of life have I restricted my growth because of gravity thinking?
- Which areas of my life am I living as though chains are still controlling my pace and direction?
- In these areas I have identified, what does living higher look like to me and am I ready to defy the gravity restrictions on my life?

— CHAPTER SIX —

ABNORMAL KIND
OF NORMAL

ABNORMAL KIND OF NORMAL

With the ending of our marriage, I was faced with the "Triple F" decision. I could either *Fight, Fly* or *Forgive*. I certainly had reason enough to do the first, opportunities to do the second, and no inclination at all to do the third!

I knew the theory. I knew the God perspective. I knew what my heart was telling me to do. I knew the right thing to do. But at this moment, when forgiveness was most needed, it felt ludicrous and unfair, as if it was mocking me.

Perhaps if I had been living in a middle eastern village wearing long robes and carrying a scroll, it may have felt more like a fit—but now? In the 21st century? After all this? Before an apology, a turnaround, or compensation? You must be kidding! How will forgiveness benefit anyone? How will it make my world better?

> *God's perspective is often like a spiritual spanner thrown into the works of natural instincts!*

When our conscience and heart require something different from us than our natural instincts, we can know for sure that the spiritual has met the natural and both are vying for our attention.

The most asked important yet vulnerable question that whispered continuously inside my mind at this time was, "Do I know better than God and so ignore him; or will I open my heart to trust him?" What I was offered by God was not a spanner but a tool to remove the chain—a tool called forgiveness.

Years later, I sat in my lounge room chatting with my close friend. Our experiences had been hauntingly similar and we had been drawn together through empathy, raw honesty, and the questions our lives raised.

This day we shared our unique sense of empowerment—not over another person but rather over our own natural instincts as we discussed what forgiveness looked like for us; how unnatural it had been to implement; and yet how free we both felt.

As we learnt to release pain, we had begun to create space in our souls to experience healing emotions. We both received valued counsel for the things we took responsibility for, and freed ourselves from those that were not. We laughed at ourselves, at humorous things both related and unrelated to our sad pasts. We strengthened ourselves spiritually by being in church and around people we wanted to emulate; people who would encourage us and urge us forward. We visited culturally interesting galleries, socially enriching events, and soul nurturing places (like the beach, shopping malls and interesting small towns). This was how we began to defy gravity.

Interestingly, we were both accused of laughing too much in our first year of divorce! Those who do not understand the nature of forgiveness or the nature of seasons seem to easily place themselves as judge over our lives! These onlookers will perhaps never know the exquisite joy that can be squeezed out of excruciating and once debilitating pain. I had said to her, "This is not normal, is it?" She had responded, "What is normal? Perhaps we will make our own normal." As we reminisced that day in my lounge room, we realized that we had!

Is Christianity, then, a "roll over and play dead," "lie down like a doormat," "grin and bear it," "smile and fake it" lifestyle? No, if it was, my friend and I would not have made it! Those phoney postures make a mockery out of humility (unforced and controlled strength) and are an insult to the justice of God.

> *Christianity is strength of character, resolve of belief, convictions of steel, heart that is pliable, mind that is teachable . . . thus providing a foundation sufficiently stable from which life can be launched.*

The ancient writer of the New Testament book of Hebrews cautioned against the emotion/attitude of bitterness. He said that it would ultimately defile a person.[11] He was passionately imploring his readers to live God's grace. He explained to them that if they fail to do so, either by not feeling worthy or by not thinking they need it, they will always hold others at arm's length from the gift of grace as well. He knew that they wouldn't be able to extend grace to another if they failed to live in grace themselves.

As I read this wisdom in the stark gloom of being newly separated it became a warning flag and a signpost for me. During that first traumatic year as a single mum, I began to look closely at my base instinctive responses to all that had happened, and at the fall out. I shocked myself with all I was capable of thinking and saying.

What comes naturally doesn't require too much effort! We won't struggle with mustering up anger, frustration, and revenge! We won't have to work at being cold with our words and hot under our collar! It doesn't take any personal integrity to soak up all our well meaning friends' sympathies and defending opinions. But if this is predominately all our circle of friends is offering, maybe we need to get a bigger circle!

We become like the friends we keep and our colloquial narrow thinking causes us to think that everyone but us is a bit off beat! Our restrictions become disguised by our own pride and self-justification and so we live according to the law of gravity . . . We live grounded.

A Bible poet described himself as a companion (friend, partner, associate, bound to those of like-mindedness, and purpose) of all who respect God and of those who keep his words.[12]

It is too easy to slip into a denying or defending environment. But beware, before long those who once knew you will hardly recognize you as you sacrifice your personal worth and dignity on the crucifix of justification. Taking denial, defense, and such self-justification street is the short road to Stuckville. After a shoulder to lean on, we need a hand to help lift us up. Hang on to and value the friend who will, in love, challenge you, be honest with you, and invest in you. As the saying goes . . . short-term pain for long-term gain.

Within our heart, God has planted seeds of trust and faith—they are his gifts to us. We don't think too much about trusting our hearts to beat and our lungs to fill with air. In the same way, we can also learn to trust God's guidance within us. This guidance helps us access his perspective and kingdom principles which touch both the physical and spiritual realms, encompassing the present, and the future. Remember, we are talking about a Plan A, God!

Learning to trust God's divine guidance fuels our antigravity thinking. It opens our eyes to new perspectives which eventually enables us to create our new kind of normal and live our best days now!

TRUSTING

Within a few months of our initial separation, my world had spiraled into the darkness of lost hope and betrayed trust. Maybe you know this feeling all too well. A victim always thinks the world has taken control. But a world without hope and trust is unreliable, unfruitful, undisciplined, and uninhabitable.

I felt like an alien in my own world and I don't think others felt overly safe there for a while either. To take back control is to truly trust—not in people, not in money, not in good fortune, and not in our own instincts, but in God. During this time, I never stopped believing in God and I never stopped loving him, but it was difficult to keep trusting him when my own instincts kept screaming out for self-satisfaction and instant results.

When the survival instinct kicks in, it's all systems go—find a job (or two or three), make a plan, write a budget, do what rewards me, put up a boundary, lock up my heart, focus on getting ahead! Conscious of those survival instinct reactions,

I still managed to make a simple decision to place my hand in his as the only sure safeguard against living a life too narrow for love and too short for vision.

I attended to the things that were important (my kids' needs, their schooling, our emotional, and physical well-being, etc.) and to the things that were urgent (working, paying the bills, etc.) and then I made room in my heart to trust God for the rest.

Around this time, I received a mind picture . . . A vision.

I was in our church auditorium helping to rearrange pots, plants, and pictures. As I do with interior design, I stood imagining how a clay pot would look by the inside entrance. I became transfixed in a potentially creative moment when I saw it.

As I was engrossed in the creative employ, I saw the clay pot as a magnificent and expensive Ming Dynasty vase on a matching pedestal. From a distance and from the outside, its glazed images and color looked perfect but a glance from above peering down into the inside revealed several hundred cracks from falls or breaks that had been over time lovingly or desperately glued back together. Every detail had been considered in its repair in an effort to maintain its perfect outward appearance.

Then I saw it topple. It wasn't pushed, knocked, or touched but it overbalanced and fell off its pedestal to the floor. Then I saw him. Jesus walked toward me unperturbed by the scene and lovingly saying, "You can't fix it this time. Leave it off the pedestal. Leave it to me. If you'll allow me to rest here on the pedestal, I'll take full responsibility for the vase and relieve you of the pain and effort of having to carefully try to mend it again."

I can remember brushing away the hot tears that filled my eyes as I saw how accurate this picture really was. Me—the mender of all things broken; me—Miss-keep-it-looking-perfect was not looking so perfect and could not fix it this time.

Now out of the mind picture and into my real world, the vase returned to the clay pot and I suddenly felt the weight of the last seventeen years. I then made a decision that defied natural logic. I chose to replace the burdensome work of restoration (both of me and my marriage) with trust in the only one who willingly takes on that sort of baggage. I was, in fact, declaring that this was a day of surrender.

That was the day I put it down, left it alone, and felt no guilt from leaving it be.

Raising hands into the air is the universal sign of surrender. In wartime, captives with no options before them surrender to their captors with hands raised in surrender submitting their lives into the hands of another. Trusting God with the details of our today, tomorrows and eternity requires a surrender. It is consenting to be captured by the love of our father in heaven and trusting in his integrity and belief in our future to see us through every bad day and every good day.

When I was a little girl, I trusted my daddy implicitly. I would often raise my hands signaling my desire to be picked up. I wanted him to pick me up, perhaps to sit on his shoulders where I would be able to see what he saw. My own boys did the same, even if sometimes out of fear or insecurity. Settled on mummy's hip and nestled into her side was a place of safety.

James had an early habit of raising his hands and pleading "up-a-mummy" (translated "can you pick me up mummy?"). Matt would run to me with huge smile and arms totally outstretched. They both did so to be close, to see what I saw and always in trust, and knowing they were loved.

Surrendering and trusting now marked my days. Why trust him? I think simply because he's been there. It started in Bethlehem where he shivered against the cold and slept in a bed meant for animal's food. In Nazareth, he grew up, paid bills, built friendships, was misunderstood, and thrown out of town. In Jerusalem, he stared down the pious, silenced the critics, stood up for the abused, was ridiculed, spoke up for the minority, was wrongfully accused, sentenced in a kangaroo court, and then led to his death. He lived his life for humanity—for us; and died for humanity—for us. Our desire to strengthen our faith is our greatest gift to him. Trust him to raise you up to see what he sees.

This begins by . . .

being prepared to risk trusting Someone we cannot see to change circumstances we cannot control.

Principle—A simple conscious decision to place our life in His hands is the only sure way to safe-guard against living a life too narrow for love and too short for vision.

- I recognise that I have worked very hard to keep up appearances and am aware of my resulting weariness.
- I accept that surrendering my life to God will impact my energy levels, my emotional welfare and my outlook for the future in positive and healthy ways.
- I realize that such surrender leaves me in a place of personal freedom without robbing me of a sense of personal responsibility.
- I am prepared to risk trusting Someone I cannot see to change circumstances I cannot control.
- Although I have nothing to lose, there are things I need to surrender and I am now choosing to acknowledge those things.

PERSONAL BEST

As a schoolgirl, I was a short-distance, record-breaking sprinter. My dad even into his retirement years was a national medal holding long distance runner. Now as an adult in life, I wanted to be a long-distance contestant too. I wanted to be able to go the distance, do the hard yards, break the runner's wall barrier, and finish well in my life. I desperately did not want my crises to define me and I desperately did not want them to represent my future.

A heaviness hovered over my little house, my little car, my finances, and my work. I needed to see past the darkness and get a glimpse of light, just a glimpse. Although I couldn't see my dreams, I could feel them. I realized I had encountered a roadblock and that I needed to be in better condition and be better resourced to compete well and get a personal best out of this life.

After the divorce, I moved us into a small but neat town house in a secure gated community. I drove a cheap car for which I worked two jobs to finance and I shopped for myself in secondhand clothing stores. Consumed with victim mentality (which I was for some time largely unaware) and now in a place as a result of decisions others made for me, I desperately needed an exit route, a bridge that would take me from hurt to wholeness; from second best to best; from surviving to thriving.

Now aware of the bitterness-versus-grace dynamic, I realized two things . . . first, I had to choose the grace path of forgiveness and, second, if I didn't, I would barricade my heart from God's grace toward me!

Choosing the temporary safety of such a barricade is pretty grim and embarrassing. Bitterness easily finds fertile soil in our souls, inadvertently sabotaging our lives as well as inflicting its nastiness on others! Such a barricaded heart can't absorb God's love and grace. And so may never be awakened to true purpose.

Bitterness announces itself to people in our world as "Look out!"; "Duck for cover!"; "Here he comes again!"; "Guess what she'll want to talk about!"; "I really can't cope with him today!" The sad thing is others whisper and we are the last to recognize what bitterness has done to us.

For me, I could neither help nor change the past—but I could help and change my responses to it. I could perhaps begin afresh, create a clear path and still get a personal best out of this. And so can you.

HURT HEART OR BITTER SPIRIT?

And so I came to the place of seeing no other option but to begin to clear the path for myself and other long-distance runners (including my kids) coming behind me. I wanted none to trip and fall; none to step in a hole or sprain an ankle. And most importantly, I wanted to finish well.

Ultimately, we all need to come to that place where we realize that life is bigger than us and that the decisions we make effect many more than just ourselves. The people in our world are relying on the fact that we will know this and live accordingly.

You know the saying, "It never rains but it pours"? Well, immediately following this profound insight into the benefits of trust and forgiveness, the weight of starting life again exponentially increased! Just when I didn't have any money, everything started to break down, wear out, or need replacing. Sound familiar?

On one particularly bad day, I can remember crying out to God in sheer frustration and desperation, "Lord I cannot fix this. I don't have the answers, resources, or energy. I am drained from the tears, the tension, and the turmoil. You are God and I am not. But you have promised wisdom for those who will ask; insight for those who will see and guidance for those who will trust. I need all three so I open my heart to allow your energy and perspective to bring something noble and good from my life. And I suggest that you do this before I scream again, lose it or do something stupid out of sheer frustration and desperation!"

That day nothing changed—but I had. When we get tested by circumstances, we soon find out what's in our heart.

The road clearing tool I needed was forgiveness . . . forgiving God for not making it all better; forgiving myself for not fulfilling the "us" family dream I had for my kids; forgiving others for betraying me and turning my world upside-down.

> *A hurt heart is the sum total of lingering memories of wounds incurred from people and circumstances throughout life. We cannot avoid a hurt heart. A bitter spirit is a result of revisiting and replaying the memories over and over, each time changing the scenario to either incur hurt or revenge on another or to punish ourselves. We can avoid a bitter spirit.*

A hurt heart is inevitable. If we live in the world and have contact with people, we will get one some time. We can't avoid a hurt heart. But we can avoid a bitter spirit—memories that linger too long, poison too many conversations, isolate too many people, and whittle away too many dreams.

I am writing this eleven years on from the events that led me on the journey of discovering the power of forgiveness, I am still tender with memories but my heart holds no bitterness. Instead, it has become a well of wisdom, understanding, and resolve out of which I have the resource to write such a book. I do not say this as a boast, but I can say it as a truth.

> **Principle—Hurt hearts which forgive become wells of wisdom, understanding, and resource.**
>
> - I choose to face both old and new pain in which people or events have caused anger or sorrow.
> - My desire for a clear path and a fresh start is now greater than my desire to keep fighting.
> - I am going to learn to recognize the markers and identifiers within myself which will alert me to bitterness and I am going to learn how not to confuse bitterness and hurt.
> - I realize that people will leave me, lie to me, cheat on me, divorce me, use me, and let me down; but I also recognize that God never will.

GROWTH THROUGH PROCESSED CHANGE

— CHAPTER SEVEN —

GROWTH THROUGH PROCESSED CHANGE

*Don't look for shortcuts to God.
The market is flooded with sure fire, easygoing
formulas for a successful life that can be practiced
in our spare time. Don't fall for that stuff, even
though crowds of people do. The way to life—to God—is
vigorous and requires total attention . . .
They are foundational words, words to build
a life on. If we work these words into our life, we are
like a smart carpenter who built his house on
solid rock. Rain poured down, the river flooded,
a tornado hit—but nothing moved that house.
It was fixed to the rock.*

*These are the wise words of Jesus as recorded
by a tax-official in the New Testament.*[13]

God's promise is that we can be unmovable in any kind of storm if we will build our life on his bedrock words.

Our spirit . . . the core of our being . . . is often called the guidance centre of life. The spirit of God whispers, nudges, illuminates, brings comfort, wisdom, clarity, conviction, and understanding to our hearts and minds. We sense his will and heart predominantly through our heart, our conscience, and through reading his word. My mother used to say that the conscience is the microphone of the spirit of God.

However, it is usual that our mind, not our spirit, is the driving force of our life. Our mind will direct our decisions, plans, actions and words. No matter how much guidance we perceive through our heart, conscience and Bible reading, if our mind says, "that's ridiculous"; "that doesn't make sense"; "that's not fair"; "that's too hard"; "that doesn't register as normal"; "I don't want to do that," then we will naturally go with what our mind dictates despite what we sense in our heart.

So when learning to apply God's life principles, our mind will often stubbornly rebel because we have programmed it otherwise and it will take time to teach it new ways of thinking. We most often have to undertake a process of building new information blocks into our mind to align our thinking with God's character and perspectives. Or in Bible-speak, we must resist becoming well-adjusted or conforming to an old culture and way of thinking and doing.[14]

Conforming has to do with outward adjustments of molding and flexing to look the part or fit the scene in order to appear "normal." Transforming, on the other hand, required a move away from "normal." It is an inner metamorphism where the change is affected by internal mechanisms that take on a life of their own.

Positive thinking experts call it neuro-linguistic-reprograming or NLR:—"neuro" referring to the brain, "linguistic" referring to the tongue or speech, and "reprogramming" referring to altering how our brain is conditioned to think. So in other words, we can reprogram the way we think by speaking differently. This begins by attaining new insights, revelation, and information that turn the light on in different areas of our life or convinces us to try something new. A new conviction or hope will stir us to speak new realities and possibilities into our own life consistently enough to change the way we think. Thinking differently will alter the way we behave because our decisions will be influenced by our new thoughts. Behaving differently will alter the response we get from the world around us.

In the early days, my existing linguistic programming had me struggling to earn a good wage; working twice as hard and never getting ahead. I was continually reminding myself that I was a single mum, a statistic, and sometimes a target. This internal dialogue repeated and underlined my weaknesses while invalidating my dreams.

Then I got a fresh picture. I was born on purpose, with purpose, and for purpose! Those dreams were mine! I didn't just want a better life, I deserved it! I did have what it took to defy the gravitational pull of circumstances.

The moment I refused to think like a victim was the same moment I began to behave like a confident winner. The town house we rented didn't usually take pets but we were able to move in with our boarder collie; I made an appointment with the state chief for oral health who did not take appointments and got one (and got the job!); I shopped where I couldn't afford the prices and found the "never to be repeated sales"; I cut my emotional and financial dependence from my ex-husband and fostered a healthy relationship between this man and his sons.

In short, my life changed as I began transforming my life from the inside by speaking differently to myself about myself.

Cultures, social prejudices, political agendas, and religious views are all influenced by this method and all use this method to influence. The ultimate outcome of course is for us to see different results and align our experiences (what we've got) with our true desires (what we want) to see and then live our positive and progressive future.

It is important to know that logic is not enough. Our minds are also influenced by our emotions or the way we feel. We don't *think* hurt, we *feel* hurt. (This is why we find ourselves doing or saying things in the heat of the moment that we may regret later when we have had time to think things through.)

Because the memory part of the brain can cause us to feel the hurt of past events as if they were happening today, we will sometimes bring past events and pain into the present and continue to allow them to invade our life and rob us of joy. The same applies to good memories . . . their impact can linger for years and years.

I can still smell the yellow and orange tinged roses in my parents' garden when I was twelve years old. I can still taste the prized few white fleshed nectarines that grew on the tree each summer in our back yard while I was growing up. I can still feel the sting of that smack I got for swearing at my brother from high up the apricot tree. I can recall the painful drawn out labor of giving birth twice and the joy of holding both boys in my arms for the first time. I can still taste my grandpa's meat patties, smell my great aunt's perfume, and hear my dad's highly exaggerated Bible stories.

Bringing experiences and events of the past into the present can be an enriching part of a family's traditions. Stories from grandparents to grandchildren can bond and locate generations in their unique place in history and leave imprints and legacies. Family legacies are not only a bequest of personal belongings or property but an invaluable and lasting gift as one generation positively influences the next.

My elder son recently messaged my parents on his return journey home after squeezing in a flying visit with them at the tail end of a business trip. My mum read me his words which went something like this: *"It was good to see you again. It's always good to see you. Sorry it was so rushed. You are the best grandparents anyone could ever wish for. Me and Matt (his brother) are grateful for the legacy of faith you have passed down to us and we live to honor you and make you proud."*

They already do.

LEGACY

We are caught in an inescapable network of mutuality, tied in a single garment of destiny. Whatever effects one directly affects all indirectly.

Martin Luther King

Philip and I have, over a number of years, been very mindful of what we are sowing into our children and others in our sphere of influence with our words and by the way we do life individually and together. We know that themes, traditions, culture, and faith leave deep imprints and etch their way into hearts, so we are actively saying, "How are we doing at clearing the path for other runners on the journey?"

But bringing the past into the present can also be a debilitating choice and one that also leaves a legacy. Two thousand years ago, these words were penned: *"The world is unprincipled. It's dog-eat-dog out there! The world doesn't fight fair. But we don't live or fight our battles that way—never have and never will. The tools of our trade aren't for marketing or manipulation, but they are for demolishing that entire massively corrupt culture. We use our powerful God-tools for smashing warped philosophies, tearing down barriers erected against the truth of God, fitting every loose thought and emotion and impulse into the structure of life shaped by Christ. Our tools are ready at hand for clearing the ground of every obstruction and building lives of obedience into maturity."*[15]

In my introduction, I alluded to the fact that God has provided us with bridges that become our exit routes when the world doesn't fight fair—exit routes away from delays, roadblocks and potential collisions that living in the past can cause . . . bridges that can help us move positively forward and literally avoid potential years of delay and hold ups. One such bridge is forgiveness. It takes us from "hurt" to "whole."

Forgiveness is powerful. It helps to shift and alter old patterns of thinking. It helps us strain out all that we don't want passed on as our legacy. It smashes warped philosophies and tears down barriers erected against God's truth. It helps us fit every loose thought, emotion, and impulse into the structure of a life shaped by Christ.

That place called Stuckville? Forgiveness gets us out of there.

Contrary to popular thought, forgiveness is not all about what we do for someone else. It's something we do firstly for ourselves. The ripple effects that create a path and form our legacy come from our own decisions and actions.

In the beginning, making the choice to forgive another may seem impossible. At the very least, it will seem difficult and the path of most resistance. It feels more natural not to go there because it crosses our natural inclinations and demands gravity defying actions. Forgiveness takes courage and determination and requires us to dig deep to find the strength we need.

The strange thing about forgiveness is that
it's not about what 'feels' right or wrong.
In fact, it's not about feelings at all.
We give it to ourselves whether we feel we deserve
it or not and we give to others
whether we feel they deserve it or not.

Here is the complication. We can make the decision to forgive, expecting some instant, accompanying satisfaction. Then, when such a feeling doesn't come, it hardly seems to have been worth our while. Such disappointment is compounded when our own personal feelings, memories, and circumstances are still in our face, keeping us awake at night!

Forgiveness is perhaps the hardest human
virtue to initiate—but initiating it is perhaps the
only way we discover its power.

And it's perhaps the most difficult of all principles to quantify or measure because the outcomes are being felt in the hearts of others (unseen), affecting outcomes for our future (unseen) or producing personal character building substance (unseen). So it becomes an unconditional choice and step of faith that we make trusting in God's judgment, that he understands our circumstances, loves us, and believes in our future.

Having said that forgiveness is not about feelings,
it's also important to say that forgiveness
is not some mechanical or robotic response that somehow
masks the issues and helps us to escape into a
state of denial.

Neither is it stupid or blind faith that is only reliant on a formula of the right words or positive thinking. Of course the right words and positive thinking cannot be separated from the process of forgiveness but they are keys not the door.

One Monty Python movie brilliantly depicts such a ridiculous scene of mere positive thinking. Did you ever see it? Two knights are fighting it out in the woods; one being hopelessly overpowered by the other. With each limb severed from his torso by the quick bladed stronger knight, the weaker yells to his opponent taunts like "Come on, is that the best you can do, I'm okay, it's just a flesh wound!" While he bled to death!

So rather than a robotic formula designed to produce instant results, the choice to forgive is the ultimate choice to take personal responsibility and take back control of our life.

THE GREAT RESCUE MISSION

Because forgiveness is a vehicle through which GRACE (undeserved favor) is offered and GRACE (undeserved favor) is received, it cooperates with a force that is neither connected to, nor reliant on, the behavior of others.

Through forgiveness, we take back control of our own life, unaffected by the natural weights and scales of payback, revenge and self-preservation.

Two thousand years ago, in the ultimate act of forgiveness, Jesus came as God's great rescue mission for humankind. His life demonstrated God's desires for relationship with us. His purpose was to point out that we had erected barriers of sin and religion that were separating us from God.

Then he became the one who tore down and destroyed those barriers. Before all humanity knew it, before they were sorry and before they even received him, he died on a Roman cross, the cruelest form of death known to man, as the ultimate sacrifice for sin—yours and mine.

Jesus died flanked by two criminals who were also crucified that day. Grace was offered. A thief crucified on one side cursed him and rejected humanity's greatest gift. A criminal crucified on the other side surrendered. Grace was extended, forgiveness was received.[16]

When grace is rejected, so is forgiveness. Thus we take on the title "victim" for whom life is "unfair." Nothing will be our fault anymore . . . not our attitude, actions, inactivity, passiveness, aggressiveness, grief, depression, overprotection, distance, or coldness. Nothing will be our fault and everything will be justifiable.

This is uptown Stuckville.

Taking responsibility and taking back control requires facing difficult facts and asking difficult questions like "How did I get to this point?"; "Where do I really want to be?"; "What and who is likely to help get me there?"; "What caused me to become indifferent?"; and "If I had to stay as I am right at this moment forever, would I be happy?"

This is part of the process of building new information software for our brain as we align our thinking with God's. It may involve:

- *Waiting* patiently instead of jumping in
- *Seeking* good counsel and mentoring
- *Extending* ourselves to help another even when our resources are limited
- *Restraining* where we would normally lash out
- *Accountablility* to a responsible "other" instead of being a lone ranger
- *Generousity* where stinginess reigned before
- *Resisting* the urge to self defend or dish out blame.

Faith (believing God) is not reliant on the object of its focus . . . that is, the thing we most want (restored relationship, increased finances, changed behavior, promotion, etc.) but on God being who he says he is.

- *All knowing* (being able to see the end of our story from the beginning)
- *Able* (being able to do more abundantly than we ever hoped or dreamed
- *Loving* (unconditionally, unreservedly and personally)
- *Reliable* (through all circumstances)

- *Faithful* (promising to never leave us or abandon us)
- *Honest* (the truth revealer in our situation) and
- *Committed* (100% to our journey)

FOR THOSE WHOSE DAYS ARE BOOK-ENDED WITH BROKEN HEARTS AND FRACTURED DREAMS

The process of forgiveness will give rise to some of our most challenging questions and will give voice to some of the most neglected and undeveloped orphans of our soul.

Here are some of the penetrating questions that you may find yourself asking:

- "What is my thought life telling about me?"
- "When did I stop having my own opinion?"
- "When did I start thinking that I don't deserve happiness?"
- "When did my spirit start to sour?"
- "When did I stop dreaming about my childhood visions?"
- "When did I stop encouraging others and facilitating their visions?"
- "When did I stop treating and pampering myself?"
- "When did I stop loving me?"
- "When did I stop advancing and start retreating?"
- "When did I stop valuing my gift of life?"
- "When did I last experience God's gift of grace or offer it to another?"
- "What am I doing to clear my own path?"

Maybe we've mastered how to hide our pain and have fooled everyone. Maybe we haven't even tried. Maybe we have always been on the edge but never in the circle. Maybe we have been on the outside looking in and everyone knows it. Maybe we never got chosen.

My pain was in being chosen but then rejected.

I knew what it was like at school when the captain would choose the fastest, most skilled, most agile with the most runs on the board to play in the team. Equally embarrassing and awkward as that of not being chosen was being chosen and then replaced midgame by a more "skilled" player.

If you nodded or sighed with understanding when you read that, then this message is definitely for you.

The most gut wrenching cry of abandonment and loneliness in all of history didn't come from a widow, an orphan on the streets, a parent losing a child, a patient in hospital, or a victim of war. It came from a cross erected on a hill in Judea. It came from Jesus of Nazareth, the Messiah. Never before nor since have such words pierced the skies and carried so much hurt. "My God, My God, why have you forsaken me?" [17]

Silence.

Jesus took upon himself the weights and scales of payback and restitution. This act separated him from his father for the first and only time. Sin and perfect love cannot be joined; they repel one another like two opposing magnets. The ripping of spirit from spirit climaxed in the air of darkness and silence that was once filled with light and the father's voice.

Silence.

No immediate answer was felt in his torn, tortured, and bleeding body. No immediate answer was seen by his distraught, pleading, and helpless mother. No immediate answer was revealed to humanity. And although no immediate answer may come to you and no immediate problem solved, he who was also once alone, he who knows abandonment, rejection and pain; he who knows you, hears and understands.

But the answers were on their way through that suffering and are here now because he chose you instead of a Plan B last minute rescue mission from God to save himself.

The miracle of this monumental act of forgiveness stretches through time and space to include you and me. Its multidimensional grasp draws us from the past, encompasses our present, and sweeps us into the eternal. How? Because he didn't stay dead! The opposing and repelling force of sin—yours and mine—had its power removed through his forgiveness. And through his resurrection, we are invited to join him in new life—with him for now and with him for eternity.

So before answering some of those challenging questions, it's good to remind ourselves that it is okay to grieve the hurts and wrongs in life as they happen. In fact, repressed hurt and anger is often more destructive than expressed anger because the former eats away at us and subtly kills us from the inside.

Then, after pausing to remember our hurts, we refuse to drag them any further, remember that God's Plan A is to take us beyond what we have known into the realm of extreme possibilities. And so when we answer our questions, answer knowing we are not alone. Answer knowing that this too will pass. Answer knowing that new life is available. Answer knowing that some answers are still a little way off. But most of all, we answer without expending all our energy trying to figure out the cause of our pain but rather, deciding how we will respond.

NO PLAN FOR PLAN B

There was no second best in God's great rescue mission for humanity.

In the heart and mind of God, from the beginning of time, there was a plan, a covenant and a fail-safe mechanism in place which would never depend on our being perfect.

It is a fail-safe covenant of relationship so that, even when we fail, we're still safe! Why? It was never about you or me being perfect. It was never about us being good enough or doing impressive things.

God established this before he even began creating the world. He did it before he created people and he did it before the people had a chance to use their free will and reject him in so doing. Our reliance on all he did would always be enough for us. Reliance on all he has done to clear our path to him is enough for us today.

So we can put away all our gold medals, certificates, and trophies and stop flexing our muscles. Equally, we must also put aside all the failures, regrets, lost hopes, and mistakes because this story is not about what we've done but what he's done; it's not about who we are but whose we are.

Principle—Forgiveness bridges the way from hurt to wholeness.

- I accept the truth that God comes to me with the grace of forgiveness which removes my sin and guilt.

- I now pray: Father God, I am overwhelmed knowing that all guilt is removed from my life simply by believing that Jesus built the ultimate bridge for me. I accept the forgiveness you offer me. Thank you for bringing me into your family. I willingly surrender to your rules of life knowing that they are for my greater good. Pick me up so I can see what you see. Show me your view and help me to change the ripple effects of my life to leave a wake of blessing and a legacy of hope. Make something good and noble of my life so that it will point the people I influence to you. With all my heart, Amen.

INTERNAL VOWS
(LINING UP OUR THINKING WITH GOD'S THINKING)

INTERNAL VOWS
(LINING UP OUR THINKING WITH GOD'S THINKING)

When we take responsibility for our actions, we can trust God with the outcomes.

Like many other life-giving principles, faith is involved in the act of forgiveness.

- When we are offering forgiveness to others, it's stating by faith that God is fair and he will do what is right—without our help! Hands off! Release it! Put it down! Leave the outcome to God!

- And when it comes to forgiving ourselves, it's stating that God is true and that his words of love and purpose for us still stand—with our help! Hands on! Pick up the responsibility! Take ownership of it! Make the changes necessary! Begin to become the person who attracts the things desired and who makes room for God to move. Here's how it works:

HANDS OFF:

When it comes to forgiving others, we need to take a giant step of faith by acknowledging God's take on forgiveness. When he forgives us, the act is so thorough that the memory of what he has forgiven is "removed as far as the east is from the west." [18]

When Jesus stretched out his arms and became nailed to his cross, he took on sin—yours, mine, and everyone else's—and won! Tucked into that extraordinary victory is the gift of forgiveness.

Perhaps it is easy to love this picture of the gift of forgiveness when it comes to our own shortcomings but we are perhaps a little suspicious of God's understanding of the true picture when it comes to forgiving others. We think God is a little short-sighted and soft at times and needs our help in administering justice, discipline, or truth. When we are tempted to do this, we need to remember that he sees the bigger picture—both ours and theirs. God works outside of our time frames, constraints, and observable realities in his response to our decision to forgive another. Offering forgiveness to another means the responsibility and weight of their actions and consequences has left our hands and now safely and surely rests with him.

For me it looked like stepping back from rushing into some decisions; it meant relinquishing control of peripheral or trivial matters; and it meant giving up wanting to know about the others' responses and behavior.

It's like charitable giving. We do it then we step back from it. Once it has left our hands, it ceases to be our responsibility. We can't control its function. Rather, trusting in the ripple effects of giving and the strong threads that tie life's heart moments together, we release all personal ownership of both our pain and of our subsequent decision to forgive . . . and we leave the outcomes to God.

HANDS ON:

But before reaching the point of healing, we first must receive forgiveness for ourselves. And here is where the work starts!

It is important not to confuse this with working for God's approval or favor. We already have that. Rather, receiving forgiveness for ourselves is more along the lines of entering into a divine cooperation.

This divine cooperation is a process of learning to align our life with God's character and his work in us. It is a combination of tapping in to God's life principles and using common sense. As an old proverb says, "Call on God but row away from the rocks."

Apostle Paul wrote an interesting piece of advice to a group of new believers who comprised the fledgling Christian church 2,000 years ago. His words point to three areas of personal responsibility needed to take God's exit route from Stuckville and to start to live out our best days.

He told these young Christians that the fight against pain and hurt was not with fists and weapons but with a trilogy of internal disciplines . . . first, they had to fight negative thinking (he called them strong-holds); second, they had to recognize truth and stand for it (the truth often opposes the presenting facts); third, they had to align their thoughts and words with that truth (he uses the military language of taking misaligned thoughts captive).[19]

Let's look at them a little closer:

1.   Internal Discipline One—PULLING DOWN STRONGHOLDS

Apostle Paul used a Greek word to describe negative patterns of thinking or strongholds. Translated, we get a picture of the mind being a house of thoughts. So who is occupying our house of thoughts? Or what are we constantly thinking about and what does that say about our life?

For six years, I lived next door to a friendly and quite generous single mother of two. She looked considerably older than her midlife years with her skin, hair, conversation, and patterns of life all bearing witness to lost dreams, raped hope, and trampled dignity. Ashamedly, I would often avoid running into her knowing well that our conversation would spiral downward to the man who had wronged her, the regrettable life she was doomed to live, and the unavoidable affect of that life on her kids.

Somehow this man's past actions, however wrong, were still holding her ransom and he was still somehow responsible for her life long after the marriage ended. The past with its failures, hurts, and betrayals had occupied her house of thoughts and these squatters kept her captive to events long past and people long moved on. They kept a strong hold on her way of thinking.

She had created a perpetual season of anger that (largely unbeknown to her) kept her prisoner restricting her pace, growth, and expansion and keeping her world too narrow for grace.

Her house of thoughts needed a renovation.

I love a good reno! The thought of the new replacing the old excites me and stirs creative juices that normally lay dormant. I find myself scanning design magazines taking note of color schemes and appliances. But to realize the dream, we must live through the dust! Tearing down worn bench tops, ripping up old floor coverings, and replacing dated appliances takes a lot of grit, stirs up a lot of grime, and uses a few grand!

The personal trainer at our local gym is constantly reminding us that short-term pain produces long-term gain! We hate hearing it but secretly we know it's true. Apostle Paul doesn't dumb it down for us either. He assures us that there will be a lot of short term "smashing, pulling down and bringing into line" going on for the long-term gain of a healthy thought life which leads to an overall progressive life.

In the early days of single mothering, I was constantly challenged by my own house of thoughts. Not only were there some unproductive and undermining squatters living in there (remnants of the girl victim) but I had set up some negative internal vows that I had to smash. Here are my old top ten:

1. We will be poor and will live in low-income areas.
2. My kids will suffer with me working two jobs and studying.
3. I have lost all I had worked hard for.
4. I was rejected so there must be something wrong with me.
5. I was not wanted so I must be unlovable.
6. My dreams can never be fulfilled as a divorced woman.
7. I couldn't bring my kids into a blended relationship so I will live alone.
8. I will never recover financially.
9. Whenever I sign Ms. and not Mrs. they will all be guessing about me.
10. I cannot make major decisions on my own.

Did moving to a small town house in a security-gated community make me feel less "low income"? No. Did signing school and bank forms as Ms. eventually empower me? No. I missed being Mrs. Did navigating through major decisions help me conquer being alone? No. Right or wrong I made them and hated doing it on my own every time. Did loving my boys and reaching out to others make me feel more lovable? No. But every time I pushed through an old mindset and faced new challenges, those old strongholds became diminished and lost their staying power until I could pull them down and replace them with either victories I had experienced or God's promises which sustained me. I began to journal the changes in my thinking and behavior. I suggest you do the same.

Every time I deliberately responded with forgiveness, antigravity thinking kicked in and I was able to stir myself up, keep Plan A out in front, hold my head high with value, and watch the climate of my circumstances change around me.

I journaled miraculous happenings like new appliances appearing at my house having told no one of the need, a cheque arriving in the mail covering the loss I made on the sale of the house, loan cars appearing in the driveway from concerned friends, and many other God-surprises.

Sometimes I would just smile, hiding these encouragements and affirmations away in my heart as I lay on my bed at night; other times I would fly to the phone to brag about the goodness of God through people.

I have included this little piece of my life not as a brag or a formula for having needs met instantly but as an example of the dramatic difference that ripple effects of grace makes in a life.

You don't have to pursue what you can attract! Do you want peace? Begin to attract it in your spheres of life. Do you want the woman or man of your dreams? Begin becoming the kind of person who will attract them. Do you want a better job? Become the kind of person who will be indispensable for that position. It will require change—are you ready for that? Knowing change is necessary but not making it happen is always detrimental. We might as well set our satellite navigational systems straight to Stuckville for a life of ordinary.

I began to take on the challenge of renewing the way I thought about my life and replacing my internal vows until I could speak of my ten big problem beliefs like this—

1. My little town house will have an attractive garden and reflect beauty. (I worked it so it did!)
2. My kids will benefit from the discipline and example of my work. (And they have!)
3. I will re-build our life. (Initially I worked two and three jobs to do just that!)
4. Rejection does not reflect dysfunction in me. (whew!)
5. Love is a free will choice and I cannot choose for another. (whew again!)
6. Go after the dreams anyway and trust God who gave them to me. (Go for it girl and never look back!)
7. Our growth and well-being comes first but I am keeping my heart open and ready for other developments. (I was making room for love.)
8. Work and get good counsel enabling right decision-making for today and tomorrow will benefit from it. (Legacy is important.)
9. My life will speak louder than my title. (I let go of pride and claimed back my self-confidence.)
10. I am not on my own—the phone connects me to family and friends and my own heart connects me to God. (I stayed secure in my faith and in the fact that I was building the DNA for the next season)

In short, I began becoming the person who could attract and live the life I desired.

> **Principle—When we take responsibility for our actions, we can trust God for the outcomes.**
> - As painful and confronting as it may be, I will make an honest confession of what I have allowed to take up residence in my house of thoughts.
> - Where necessary, I will seek good counsel and wisdom to help me consruct my "replacement" beliefs. An example of what that might look like would be.

CURRENT BELIEFS .... REPLACEMENT BELIEFS
Shame .... Confidence
Guilt .... Freedom from the past
Inferiority .... Equality
Regret .... Release
Disappointment .... Renewed Hope
Fear .... Boldness
Pride .... Humility
Anger .... Calmness
Paranoia .... Rationality
Selfishness .... Generosity
Stinginess .... Extravagance

2. Internal Discipline Two—DICIPHER TRUTH FROM FACTS

The second area of responsibility that Paul pointed out was the need to destroy warped philosophies that stand in defiance against truth . . . God's truth about us. It's almost military language with the thought being to interrogate what we allow into our house of thoughts. After all, it's our house!

We are to interrogate our thoughts with questions like:

- Where did you come from?
- Are you a friend of my future or an ally of the past?
- Will you help or hinder me living my best days now?
- Are you a co-worker of grace or an accomplice of revenge?
- Are you an exit route to freedom or a roadblock in my journey?
- Have you come to remind me of what went wrong or forecast what can be made right?
- Have you come to bring me peace or torment?

There exists for every believer an antagonistic relationship between the facts and the truth. Sometimes the facts will puff their chests out intimidating us and exalting themselves above God's truth about us.

Such facts might present themselves as being the truth with all the surrounding evidence of circumstances and emotions. For a sick person to believe that God has provided the gift of healing is to believe and act on that belief despite the symptoms, the medical reports, and sometimes the pain. From the outside, such faith can appear childish, irresponsible, and stupid. Yet such outrageous acts are not blind denial nor wishful thinking but a surrender to both God's divine intelligence and his guidance.

A friend of Philip's stayed beside his new born son every hour he could in a hospital ward, stroking his tiny hand, and whispering stories of their yet unlived future together. You see the baby was born with a serious condition and the medical prognosis contained very little hope. The baby received all the medical assistance offered but the father decided to inquire no further regarding his son's health. Instead he chose to speak words of affirmation, hope, future, and vision into his little ears.

What was so amazing about this experience, he later told us, was the impact it had on him as his own ears heard his own mouth make a different sound and tell a different story to the one they heard around them. He was selective regarding well-wishers who wanted to support through visitation as he safeguarded his positive environment.

His vigil included word pictures of birthday parties, football fields, Christmas, and school sports days—father and son together.

Against all odds, the baby went home with his parents. The little boy is now four years old and father and son kick the football together. Did the hospital story telling vigils make a difference? They did to the father. The facts did not line up with the desires of his heart so he went back to the source of all life—he went back to God. He deciphered his truth from the facts.

He told us, "When we get challenged by circumstances, we know what's in our heart." He knew that what was in his heart was very different to what was in his world so he began to draw out some of what was in his heart to change his world.

The Bible's signature message is Life.
When we begin by faith to speak life into our
circumstances, life responds.

Clear guidelines about the "what" and "how" of the way we speak have been given to us in the Bible.

"Finally, friends, whatever things are true, whatever things are noble, whatever things are just, whatever things are pure, whatever things are lovely, whatever things are of good report, if there is any virtue, and if there is anything praiseworthy—meditate on these things." Philippians 4:8 (New King James Version)

In a court of law, the prosecutor's responsibility is to present as much evidence and supporting facts that will give weight to an argument which he then presents as the truth.

In our physical world, we look to the facts to give weight to our opinions which we will then conclude is the truth. However, the thoughts and arguments that God presents to us through the Bible may sometimes give us a different picture of truth. While we look to the facts to give weight to our opinions, God is revealing to us his creative heart and mind giving weight to his opinions concerning us.

Sometimes, the facts—being temporary circumstances— are at odds with the overall permanent purposes for our life. In God's economy, the facts are often quite separate from the truth.

So now we are presented with two options and two questions. Do we invest all our time, energy, emotions, focus, and finance into dealing with the facts or is God's opinion also worth investigating? And do we believe only the evidence that has gathered itself around us (which takes very little effort) or do we dig deep for the courage to draw out faith and trust in something we can't see and perhaps can't feel?

Whose report will we believe? The best way to know God's report is to know his word. Only that simple trust that God is who he says he is, has what he says he has and will do what he says he will do can help us confidently "cast down every argument" that does not belong to our future—or Plan A.

Fifteen Fat Facts

In my dark and uncharted days of separation and divorce, the weight or facts concerning my life grew into loud obnoxious intruders lauding their presence over me as fifteen fat facts! They sang out their songs of doom over my life, my circumstances, and my future as I struggled to work through the "where to from here." But I couldn't deny it, they were indeed real, they were fifteen frightening fat facts and they looked like this—

1. You are a single mum
2. You are a statistic
3. You have no money
4. You have no career anymore
5. Your family is 2000 kilometers away
6. You have no house
7. You have no car
8. You have no future
9. You have lost your opportunities
10. You have lost what you worked for
11. You have lost what you believed for
12. You have very few options
13. You have a stigma attached to your status
14. You are confused
15. You will find it hard to make ends meet

The dictionary's definition of the truth is "conforming to and in line with the facts." However, God's opinions are often quite the opposite to apparent facts. I had dreams and hopes inside me that seemed to get swallowed up in what was going on around me. My single, abandoned and broke circumstances didn't look like my picture of the future at all! In fact, they made that little girl dream look impossible!

This is the place many people stop—right here, stuck in places they didn't want to be for longer than they wanted to stay; especially those who see themselves as innocent victims who are owed something. I heard a friend of mine say at the height of his "stuckness"—"Well, the God I knew and the God I am experiencing are two different things. If that's God, you can have him!" And it was back to the laws of the jungle for him.

It was back to self-sufficiency and facts. He was not prepared to action faith or wait in trust. He was not prepared to see anything more than his natural eyes could see. The facts were the only truth he was prepared to see. I have since lost contact but at least for two years I watched him move from one bad relationship to another, make the same relationship mistakes, and blame God in the same ways for allowing bad things to happen to good people.

God's word—his truth for me—didn't conform to, nor was it in line with, the facts. Which would I believe? The Old Testament poet wrote, "God's word is a lamp to my feet and a light to my path." [20] As I poured through his word to find his truth and his report, I found evidence that God was singing his song of life over me and my future. Every condemning fact had its sting removed by the truth of God's heart and words for me.

I began to transform my thinking into antigravity thoughts as I memorized his words and the theme of his heart and hummed it as a song over my life:

- I am a good woman and mother.
- I am generous with my resources.
- I will not need to borrow but I will lend to many.
- I will see my dreams fulfilled.
- God will finish what he started in me.
- I am attentive to opportunities and God is connecting my dots.
- I am loved and worthy to be loved.
- I am forgiven and can forgive.

When our thoughts are drawn upward, it's hard to look down.

Without faith, God's promises may at first appear like wishful thinking for some other person in some other time; and without trust, we will be too small and diminished to receive them for ourselves.

Faith defies gravity—everything that would pull us down and seek to keep us down. Faith is looking to God and trusting him for the outcomes of his own promises.

So here is his song of truth and life found from his word that eventually replaced my fifteen frightening fat facts:

1. He is a husband to the widow and a father to the fatherless.

   Psalm 68:5 A father of the fatherless, a defender of widows, is God in his holy habitation.

2. We can overcome because we are a child of God.

   1 John 4:4 You are of God, little children, and have overcome them, because he who is in you is greater than he who is in the world.

3. We have an inheritance.

   Colossians 1:12 . . . giving thanks to the father who has qualified us to be partakers of the inheritance of the saints in the light.

4. The steps of a good man or woman are ordered by the Lord.

   Psalm 37:23 The steps of a good man are ordered by the Lord, and he delights in his way.

5. He puts the solitary in families and makes the bound up to prosper.

   Psalm 68:6 God sets the solitary in families; He brings out those who are bound into prosperity.

6. He will restore to me the years that have been eaten away.

   Joel 2:25-27 So I will restore to you the years that the swarming locust has eaten, the crawling locust, the consuming locust and the chewing locust . . . You shall eat in plenty and be satisfied, and praise the name of the Lord your God who has dealt wondrously with you; and My people shall never be put to shame.

7. Not even one sparrow falls to the ground without God knowing it—I am more valuable to him than a bird.

   Matthew 10:29-31 Are not two sparrows sold for a copper coin? And not one of them falls to the ground apart from your Father's will . . . Do not fear therefore; you are of more value than many sparrows.

8. He knows the plans he has for me, they are for good to give me a future and a hope.

   Jeremiah 29:11 For I know the thoughts that I think toward you says the Lord, thoughts of peace and not of evil, to give you a future and a hope.

9. Sing barren woman and draw back your curtains and stretch out your boundaries; think big! You will not be put to shame!

   Isaiah 54:1-5 Sing O barren, you who have not borne! Break forth into singing and cry out loud you who have not labored with child! For more are the children of the desolate than the children of the married woman . . . Enlarge the place of your tent and let them stretch out the curtains of your dwellings; do not spare; lengthen your cords and strengthen your stakes. For you shall expand to the right and to the left, and your descendants will inherit the nations . . . Do not fear, for you will not be ashamed.

10. My eyes haven't seen or ears heard even the half of what God has prepared for me.

    1 Corinthians 2:9 Eye has not seen, nor ear heard, nor have entered into the heart of man the things which God has prepared for those who love him.

11.	He came to give me life in abundance.	*John 10:10 The thief does not come except to steal, and to kill, and to destroy. I have come that they may have life, and that they may have it more abundantly.*
12.	The end days will be better than the beginning.	*Job 8:7 Though your beginning was small, yet your latter end would increase abundantly.*
13.	He has chosen me and accepted me.	*Ephesians 1:4-5 . . . just as he chose us in him before the foundation of the world, that we should be holy and without blame before him in love, having predestined us to adoption as sons by Jesus Christ to himself . . . which he made us accepted in the beloved.*
14.	The peace of God which is beyond natural understanding will guard my heart and mind.	*Philippians 4:7 And the peace of God which surpasses all understanding, will guard your hearts and minds through Christ Jesus.*
15.	God will supply my needs in ways that are beyond me.	*Philippians 4:19 And my God shall supply all your need according to his riches in glory by Christ Jesus.*

God's inspired instruction for us is that any thought not consistent with our dreams of a better future or fulfilling our potential and creative purpose . . . in fact any thought that keeps us ragged and not radiant . . . should be thrown out and the door shut!

We Either Do Life Or Life Does Us

A period of awakening or realization to the unlawful squatters we've allowed in to set up residence in our mind will commence a season of grieving that will actually feed our value and our self worth—so long neglected, so long awaiting our attention.

It's both validating and healing to be able to honestly say:

- I cry because of the sadness.
- I hurt because of the betrayal.
- I'm diminished because of the embarrassment.
- I retreat because of the failure.
- I'm empty for lack of encouragement.
- I'm angry because of the injustice.
- I'm small from the years of abuse.
- I'm indifferent due to neglect.
- I'm disillusioned from lost hope.

These statements voice the reality of why and how things got to be the way they are.

> *Being honest says,*
> *"I'm not nuts and I'm not*
> *excessively needy nor dysfunctional.*
> *But I have been wronged and*
> *everything within me and about me*
> *has been touched by it.*
> *No wonder I allowed these thoughts in."*
> *We need to know that it's okay to*
> *recognize and express that!*

It's also okay to feel angry. Anger is a legitimate emotion. It isn't a sin any more than laughter is. We're not cautioned not to get angry but we are cautioned not to let it linger and consume us. It can become a dangerous emotion when its clean flame of reaction to wrong turns to the toxic smoke of hate, revenge, or jealousy.

So it's not just okay but healthy to recognize our emotions. Yet it can't end there or the validation becomes only an academic exercise that pats us on the back, providing justification for feeling, and being the way we are. But recognizing our emotions does not, of itself, bring along solutions and new paths.

A victim can validate his feelings and situation but still remain helplessly at the mercy of an offender having changed nothing. He or she must move on . . . must exit from this emotional dead-end. Forgiveness is our only path to restoration, recovery, and new beginnings. By showing mercy to an offender and surrendering to God's perspectives we remove ourselves from this emotional stalemate.

Now we find ourselves saying, "I am able to trust again because I chose to trust God over my own impulses."

Now we begin to impact our life rather than merely having life impact us.

- Martin Luther King did life in a dark time of America's history. His courageous and generous spirit won over a nation's racist hatred.
- Mother Teresa did life as she fought and won for so many of Calcutta's poorest and dying.
- Moses did life as he left the comforts of palace life and brought freedom to a nation.
- Every teenager who defies the statistics of the ghetto; every child who lives bravely beyond abuse; every abandoned wife who rises to meet her destiny; every man who refuses failure—these choose life and life chooses them.

**Principle—We can live being impacted
severely by life or live severely impacting life!**

- I choose to own the hurt or other consequences of
the past. It happened. It was wrong.
- I recognize the pain or dysfunction that these hurts
and consequences have caused me.
- I will take stock of my confused identity.
- I will give honor and even sympathy to myself for
living with the mental gymnastics necessary to get to
this place.
- I will find ways to pamper my exhausted soul.
- I will begin a new theme song for my life, including
self-talk which will sound less like my facts and
more like my dreams, visions, and potential.

As you employ this principle, you will be liberated by
your honesty and self-love without feeling condemned or guilty
about it.

It's time to recognize that parts of our past belong
"there" and not "here." However many fat facts you may have,
take these squatters and space invaders prisoner and tell them
very clearly that their services are no longer needed. As a
company of one, you are hereby downsizing and replacing them
with more efficient and qualified resources that will be more
conducive to your future growth and vision! Don't even give
them the golden handshake.

**3.   Internal Discipline Three—TAKING MISALIGNED
THOUGHTS CAPTIVE**

The third area of personal responsibility is to bring
every thought into captivity. The Apostle Paul declares a
war-zone—war between the natural laws of the dog-eat-dog
jungle and God's supernatural laws of going the extra mile,
loving when it hurts and giving grace to the undeserving. And in
war, there are captives!

It is not enough to interrogate the enemy; we must imprison them. Every negative, restricting, diminishing, and backward thought must become our prisoner not our ruler.

When we rule our thoughts, decisions, and actions, we become the rulers of our destiny. Ultimately, we must teach our mind what to think by reprogramming it with path clearing, roadblock demolishing and future restoring words and pictures.

As mentioned earlier, Apostle Paul says in the New Testament book of Romans 12:2 that inner transformation comes out through this renewing of mind. In other words, to become transformed from the inside out, it must start from within us—in our own minds and from a new source.

> *This is antigravity thinking. It is replacing thoughts that pull us earthward with promises that pull us heavenward, leaving behind the thoughts that drag us backward and replacing them with thoughts that compel us forward.*

Also, once we have accepted Jesus Christ as our savior and partner in life, we become brand new in a spiritual sense.

However, with this fresh beginning we don't inherit a new brain! Our life-long quest now is to teach our brain to accept new life principles from our creator God and empowering words about us and our future! In other words, we move from operating by the laws of the jungle to the laws of the kingdom.

These principles will often seem ridiculous when we compare them to our old ways of thinking. It will take time to prove them through our experiences. For example—if we want to receive, learn to be a giver; if we want to be top dog, learn to serve others; if we want more out of life, learn to give ours away; if we want wisdom, learn to be humble; if we want the top rung of the ladder, learn the significance of the bottom rung; if we want respect, discover how to value others.

God's principles are out of this world and we may think initially that they are working against us. It can look as if everyone else seems to get the better deal at our expense. Or we may say, "There is no way in the world God can do anything with this!" I'm never really sure how he does because God's methods are often beyond me. Trust him with the what and let him do the how!

God's heart is for you not against you and his methods have a way of blessing you and others in your world. His word promises to be a lamp for you in dark places, a voice to you in silent times and the truth for you in your confusion. But . . . most importantly, these principles can take your life from a "cup-half-empty" mindset to full—literally!

To forgive will go against every natural inclination in us. Unfortunately, when we need its healing force the most, forgiveness will neither seem a lovely idea nor seem an empowering one. It will push against all our natural instincts and feelings. But that's the problem, forgiveness is not a natural force.

Revenge, pay back, and getting even are the natural laws of the jungle but forgiveness is a spiritual law. So it is reasonable to conclude that the spiritual work and the results will look different at first; that they will be of a spiritual kind, not a natural, or obvious kind.

We might initially think our efforts of forgiveness are futile when we see no immediate or obvious results for ourselves or our circumstances. Or we might think our circumstances are beyond fixing. But . . .

God's how is often unfathomable and the results of healing, growth, insight, regained, confidence and wisdom are like fine-aged cheese—not three minute noodles! Give forgiveness time.

**Principle—If my thought-life shapes the way
I construct myself, then I owe it to myself to
guard my thought-life with diligence.**

- I will put my thought-life through a "medical check up." I will take stock of my dominant private thoughts about myself and my future.

- Having already learned that how I define myself will also define me, do I need to give my life a new definition?

- If "yes," I will begin to write down and use new words which are in line with my desires for the future, my dreams, and my abilities.

- I choose to see myself becoming the person who fits my dream picture of the future.

- I recognize that there are things that I need to be consistently doing to become the person who will attract those things into my life.

- I choose to trust in God's "how," embracing both my confidences any my doubts, but relying on God's grace to accept me as I am at this moment.

CHAPTER NINE

WHAT FORGIVENESS LOOKS LIKE

WHAT FORGIVENESS LOOKS LIKE

Our fascination with forward has:
- Identified Stuckville and the way out
- Found hope in the inevitability of seasonal change
- Adjusted our perspective about our immediate realities and our future and
- Brought our internal language in line with our desired future.

We are now down to the serious end of town. It is time to forgive.

Forgiveness is:
- A force
- A grace-line
- Intensely personal
- A command
- A release.

It makes sense to understand each of these layers of forgiveness and, I suggest to you, will even add strength, and courage to the process for you.

1.   FORGIVENESS IS A FORCE:

The moment we choose the forgiveness path, life will begin to change gear, and pick up pace. Why? Because whenever we put something heavy down (like responsibility belonging to someone else, past offences and self blame) that we have been carrying around for a long time, we naturally feel lighter.

As we have already established, facing forgiveness requires us to consider the emotional attachments and hurts from the past that we've been dragging behind us. It prompts us to consider honestly where they came from, why they are there—even the offences and the indescribable hurts—and what our appropriate personal response might be.

Now, the moment we choose to pick up and use the tool of forgiveness, our life will begin to change gear, and pick up pace. God knows this. He knows it's a powerful force . . . that's why he's so strong about it! He knows that refusing to receive it for ourselves or offering it to others can rob us of our dignity, time, health, happiness, confidence, influence, integrity, vision, relationships, and yes, even our eternal destiny with him!

Mysterious as it may sound, forgiveness is a force. To combat a negative force—for example prejudice or anger, we have to use a force of greater impact. To use a force of equal impact—for example to play along for the sake of keeping the peace, may cause a temporary standoff and keep things at bay for a time or maintain the status quo; but a greater force will be needed to overcome and gain victory or see change.

Forgiveness is the greater force because it carries the strength of grace. It doesn't just combat a negative force, it overpowers it, and its impact even increases with the strength of the offence. What a force!

The power of forgiveness is not used to force change upon someone else though. Its force usually impacts us long before it is manifested in others or is even seen in our circumstances. It is most magnificent when it touches and influences the world through us—changing culture, removing barriers, altering attitudes, and championing grace.

We must develop and maintain the capacity to forgive. He who is devoid of the power to forgive is devoid of the power to love. It's not merely an emotional something. Love is creative, understanding goodwill for all men. It is the refusal to defeat any individual.
Martin Luther King. JR
"Loving Our Enemies"—an extract from a sermon delivered in Alabama 1957

2.   FORGIVENESS IS A GRACE LINE:

Remember, forgiveness is not only about extending grace to others but receiving it firstly for ourselves. This is sometimes the hardest leg of the journey.

We love to give especially when it spot lights us or when it makes us feel superior, needed, or important. Such giving actually comes with an agenda and it has become about us. Sacrificial, selfless giving is the extravagant type which doesn't come with an agenda and whose focus is upon another. This type of giving is usually done behind the scenes, without accolades and at our own cost.

But did we know that receiving can also come with an agenda? When a gift is initially turned down, the point argued, and the person offended, it has also become about us! Whether it's inverted pride ("Oh, I could never receive that"); or hard core pride ("We don't need charity"); or a dysfunctional sense that receiving equals weakness or inadequacy ("I don't need your help") . . . Whatever the pride looks like, it has shut the door of grace from our receiving end and in the face of the one doing the giving.

Because life is so approval based, it is natural for us to think that our mistakes or failures have cancelled out our worthiness when it comes to receiving. Subconsciously, we can set up a grace line assessing ourselves against our behavior or personal view of value. Mostly we won't feel right or good enough and will see ourselves falling below the grace line. Depending on our self view, we will either try to figure out ways to crawl, climb, and work our way up above the grace line to God's favor, or we will see ourselves as a lost cause and give up on trying.

When we think this way, we nullify grace and make it of no effect. Contrary to anything that makes sense, God's grace cannot be earned. It is extravagant, and has no strings attached. It is a gift for all seasons which is offered to us as we are right NOW.

> *Even if you decided to rely entirely on your own power and strength to work out your life, God would not revoke your heavenly insurance policy, rub out your name or change his posture of patience toward you. Trust in this unfailing favor and outrageous generosity.*

So if we think of grace as being like a line then it must be thought of in terms of a shifting grace line. In other words, when we feel like we've fallen below the line, acknowledge our state or fault, and rely on all God has done for us, we'll find that the line has shifted to where we are!

That's God's nature. He meets us where we are right now. There are no "if you prove yourself" or "after you've shown me the change" or "here is your list of punishments." There is only, "Welcome back, I'm glad you decided to run to me and not from me."

During his time on Earth, Jesus was a master storyteller. One such story illustrates this grace line beautifully. It is known in the Christian community as the story of the Prodigal Son.[21] It goes like this.

After culturally insulting his father by requesting his inheritance and then disappearing to squander it, a young man is left destitute and penniless. He carefully prepares a speech in his head that he will deliver to his father before deciding to return home. "I will arise and go to my father and I will say to him father I have sinned against heaven and before you, and I am no longer worthy to be called your son. Make me like one of our hired servants."

He doesn't know this at the time, but his father hasn't written him off. In fact, he has been watching and waiting for his son's return. Now he sees his son in the distance. The son does not even have a chance to finish his confession before his father forgives him and calls for a celebration of joy.

In that story, Jesus perfectly illustrated the perfect line of grace—the shifting grace line that met a repentant yet undeserving and bankrupt soul.

But there is another son in the story. He stays home and works faithfully and consistently over the years. Now, hearing of this welcome home celebration, he is overheard saying, "All the years I have been here and father never threw a party for me!" The unexpected news of his brother's return and the unpalatable news of his father's unconditional forgiveness leaves a bad taste in his mouth and a sting in his heart. He resents the celebration his father has organized and refuses to go to the party.

Both sons did time in Stuckville. One was stuck in rebellion and the other was stuck in resentment. One came home to a welcome and the other stayed home and wallowed in self-pity.

When we're jealous, envious, bitter, or resentful we miss the party. We literally incarcerate ourselves in unforgiveness and chain ourselves to the walls of our self-made prison.

We need to turn down the heat before it turns to hate. And we need to deal with the hurt before it poisons our hearts.

Remember you are God's child, nothing can ever change that. Go on, go to the party, YOU know YOU want to. There's a place setting just waiting for you. Listen, can you hear the father? "Child, you are always with me, everything I have is yours anyway."

There is no sin or state too bad for God's hand to reach into; no offense too great for his heart to touch and heal. He created the ultimate grace line. Even if we've squandered our inheritance and every resource we previously had, he has paid for our return and continues to fund our dreams. That's how he demonstrates his love, his grace line moves to us.[22]

3.   FORGIVENESS IS INTENSELY PERSONAL:
Even if we could find someone who has had a mirror experience to ours, our pain will still remain unique to us. No one else will fully understand the level of intensity or degree of anguish that we have lived. No one has the right or authority to say "get over it" or demand that we forgive. This is our choice alone. We know that it is also our gift, our tool for getting unstuck and our exit route back to know we can live an incredible Plan A life.

Just as our experiences are intensely personal to us, we are intensely personal to God. Forgiving others cleanses the conscience and clears the path for unhindered relationship with God.[23]

Sometimes our pain is private—pushed to the limit by a cold or abusive spouse; segregated by race, gender, qualifications, religion, or age; compromised by a seducing or unguarded boss or empty through the loss of a new born or loved one. The world may not know . . . but we do.

Sometimes it might be public—branded by a handicap that we had no control over; marked with a disease that we never expected; labeled with a title with which circumstances now define us; landed with a divorce we didn't want; presented with a baby we didn't plan for. We can't hide because everyone knows.

Private or public, our pain is not hidden from God.

He is not waiting or expecting a public confession from us, just a private release and acknowledgement that his grace is sufficient for us. Take him with you as you journey through the deepest valleys of your personal pain and let him walk beside you as you retell the stories and events of those dark days and nights. And then see. See him with you. He never left. And then listen. He's saying something to you. You want the words to be "I love you" but you already suspect that. You want to hear "forgiven" but you sense that too. Listen carefully because what he is saying has come from the deepest places in him also.

"My grace is sufficient for you."[24]

- Grace that shivered in a tiny baby in Bethlehem laying in a bed that was built for animal's food.
- Grace that lived through the accusations that his mother was pregnant with him before she married his father.
- Grace that reached out to the unlovely, the untouchable and the unpopular.
- Grace that flourished amid disbelief, mistrust, suspicion, and hatred.
- Grace that was forged in temples enlightening stubborn religious minds.
- Grace that gave lost causes fresh beginnings.
- Grace that was purified in its submission to his father even to the point of torture and death.

And when his grace becomes sufficient for you personally, it miraculously allows it to become sufficient for others in your world. You can trust God with your emotions. He created your personality and temperament. You can trust him with your life. He gave his so yours could flourish.

Our name is known to God and our journey familiar to him. He has seen the injustice, and the unfairness. He has heard the lies, seen the cheating, and observed the cover-ups. Our wounded heart has resonated in his and our cries have been heard in heaven. Strangely, his grace has sustained us even though that truth didn't register in our broken hearts. May be it will now. And may be that knowing will breathe the confidence we need to tap into God's grace force.

Arrive at forgiveness by knowing that father's heart beats for you. Arrive at forgiveness because you never want to be separated from that. He knows it's personal.

4. FORGIVENESS IS A COMMAND:

We can be very sure that when God communicates something as a command, he is passionate about the matter. It's like a parent driving home the command for a child to look before crossing the busy road or not pulling at mummy's arm while she is driving or not diving into water where the depth is unknown.

As parents and guardians, we understand the possible consequences and serious or damaging ramifications that some behaviors can cause. It is in our hearts and for the child's safety that we demand OBEDIENCE.

It's the same with God. When he commands something, he knows the benefits attached to it; he knows the repercussions of not listening; he knows and wants what is best for us.

In the vexing matter of forgiveness, the sobering command from father God is this . . . forgive others so that he will forgive us.[25]

Failing to do so doesn't just jeopardize our happiness and future, it roadblocks our relationship and intimate friendship with God! A barricaded heart even barricades God! A choice not to forgive is a choice not to live in intimate friendship with God.

Having an intellectual knowledge that forgiveness is not reliant on feelings to initiate or for it to be effective doesn't help a great deal when we know we have been hurt by someone. The very issue is kept alive every day by our memories and feelings. What is helpful is for us to remember that God's principles are based on the force of truth. Who is truth? He is. So when God gives us his word or his truth he is giving us himself. He is laying his life on the line about the matter.

> *When divinity partners with humanity, the ordinary metamorphoses into the extraordinary.*

To believe what he says is to believe him. To believe him is to see his power of grace ignite our world. To believe him is to place our life in pretty big hands. To believe him is to trust him to do what only he can do. To believe him is to truly enter relationship.

It is also helpful to keep reminding ourselves that God's principles will often seem opposite to our natural ways of thinking and will sometimes seem unreasonable, humbling, and unfair. But if God says do it, there must be some deeper reason why we really need to.

But remember, if our physical world and God's spiritual world have collided through relationship, giving us access to his heart and mind, we also have access to his divine guidance for our journey. I have learned that it may appear in the most peculiar and unexpected ways.

Apostle Paul wrote to the new believers struggling to understand how to marry their natural responses with this new teaching:

> *We of course have plenty of wisdom to pass on to you once we get our feet on firm spiritual ground, but it's not popular wisdom, the fashionable wisdom of high priced experts that will be out of date in a year or so. God's wisdom is something mysterious that goes deep into the interior of his purposes.*

We don't find it lying around on the surface. It is not the latest message, but more like the oldest—what God determined as the way to bring out his best in us, long before we ever arrived on the scene. The experts of our day haven't a clue about what this eternal plan is. If they had, they wouldn't have killed the master of the God-designed life on a cross. That's why we have this scripture text:
No one's ever seen or heard anything like this, never so much as imagined anything quite like it—What God has arranged for those who love him.
But we've seen and heard it because God by his spirit has brought it all out into the open before us.
The spirit not content to flit around on the surface, drives into the depths of God, and brings out what God planned all along. Who ever knows what we're thinking and planning except we ourselves? The same with God—except that he not only knows what he's thinking, but he lets us in on it.
God offers a full report on the gifts of life and salvation that he is giving us. We don't have to rely on the world's guesses and opinions. We didn't learn this by reading books or going to school; we learn it from God who teaches us person to person through Jesus, and we're passing it onto you in the same first hand, personal way.
2 Corinthians 2:6-16 (Message Bible Translation)

When Christ tells us to forgive, he is often speaking to those who are most vulnerable—to those who have in some way, at some level, been hurt, violated, humiliated, and whose trust has been betrayed. Even at the point of trampled innocence, we are told to forgive.

> *We're not invited to forgive if it's our turn, or if it's fair, we're commanded to forgive so we can start flourishing.*

Don't view it grudgingly but gratefully. God is not trying to rule us with a rod, but rather reward us with a gift. He is not trying to confuse us but rather uncomplicate us. He's not trying to mess with us but give us more of himself so we get the most out of ourselves.

There is no better time to understand his mysterious heart but at a time when sorry seems to be the hardest word.

Yes, it's a command because God only knows where our life will go without it!

5. FORGIVENESS IS A RELEASE:

The dictionary defines forgiveness as *"to pardon a legitimate debt."* By very nature of the words, many people have found it impossible to forgive thinking that pardoning will dismiss the offense and allow the perpetrator to be free of responsibility. The world's judicial system agrees with God that there are consequences to our actions—that we will reap what we sow.

To pardon such a legitimate debt by no means lessens or even overlooks it. What pardoning does is releases us from the long-term entanglement of its emotional hold.

I have heard of court cases being dragged out for years with individuals pursuing justice, compensation, recompense, and vengeance for offenses committed against themselves or loved ones. Although some motives may even be warranted, I have to wonder at the time and money lost to the vendetta.

How many moments were lost to distraction? How many relationships were lost in the fight? How many people were diminished by living the past in their present? And how many individuals were swallowed up in the grief and bitterness of the fight—only to be left diminished; desperate to make up for "lost time" and unwittingly left to live out "Plan B." Does the blood money bring peace? Does the pay back bring them back? Does the lash out move anyone forward?

The very public divorces and settlements of globally famous couples draw attention to bitter fights for "rights" and hefty compensations. But money like wine can only temporarily numb their realities. Money will not heal the wounds, address the reasons, or close the hole in an angry or hurt heart.

So what eventually happens to a hurt soul who has all the convenience and comfort money can buy—traveling fist class, shopping-up-market, holidaying Europe style and eating in the finest restaurants? I think they largely do just what my friend did when he gave up on God when he equated his circumstances to being his truth.

They both use the laws of the jungle (fight, revenge, pay-back, self satisfy) to artificially create a temporary self-satisfying "truth"—it's just that money can stretch out the self satisfying bit for longer! But when the stuff no longer satisfies and the "buzz of the buy" no longer thrills, they are still in Stuckville.

My marriage breakup gave me some first-hand insight into these times. I was summonsed to court twice. I had never attended court before. It was like I was living someone else' life. The divorce needed to be legally finalized and our boys needed to be legally afforded the security and stability of their normal home life with their mum.

I assumed a posture of expecting grace so I had no intention of fighting for assets. I expected that any fair appraisal of our situation would find us deserving of the few comforts we retained. I was not interested in uncovering hidden assets or fighting for legal rights. I was from this time forward a single mother. I had at least for that moment a broken heart. Assets would not change that, things could not change that. I had a hole in my heart. Assets and things would not heal it. I put God to the test—I actioned faith and I waited in trust.

I released myself from the roller coaster of weights and balances; of "he owes, she deserves"; of "his fault, my fault." I signed out of being a victim, of being controlled, and of being inferior.

My life would now be shaped by my decisions. The path that lay before me was uncharted, unknown, and scary. I didn't know exactly what living in faith and trust would end up looking like one, five, or ten years down the track—but I also didn't know what living by instinct would look like either. (Although I had my suspicions that it wouldn't look good!) So I chose the God path and trusted that he knew what he was doing when I didn't.

In my mind, I released the one closest to me who hurt me the most. I released the attachment I had to the things. I released the offenses and betrayal leading up to this action. I released the debt owing. I released the former picture of our future. I released the past and in doing so, I released me.

WHEN GRACE IS OUTRAGEOUS

There was an article in our local paper a few years back that pierced my heart as it told the story of the shifting grace line that released two families of a debt that could never be repaid.

Two families were touched forever by a fatal car accident. One family had lost their innocent son and the other family was living the nightmare of their son's negligent and alcohol-affected driving which would lead to a sentence of manslaughter. The court case recorded an unparalleled and extreme outcome.

The grieving parents of the deceased and innocent young man tearfully pleaded before the judge on behalf of the other family for acquittal. They had arrived at forgiveness which they demonstrated before the court by saying that they had lost a son which would affect their lives forever—what possible good could come from another family suffering the same pain and losing their son? "One boy is gone," they said. "What is the sense in losing two boys?" Surprisingly the guilty boy was released from the possible hatred, vendetta, and resentment that could have haunted him for the rest of his life by those who had a "right" to do so.

The hardest aspect to face in all this is that a pardon has to do with the person not the action—it has to because the "what" came from a "who."

Although in this case the boy was spared a prison sentence, the following events and consequences became inconsequential to the family offering forgiveness. In other words, they gave up all rights to control the outcomes of the guilty boy's life. They did not demand regular paroled check-ups, performance standards, or evidence that he had learned his lesson and changed his ways; but they trusted instead in the effects of grace that forgiveness releases.

Releasing a debt is giving up all claim to compensation and trusting the outcomes of this unnatural, mysterious, and almost super human force called forgiveness. It is done so, knowing that God is loving; that he will not violate our free will; and that he is fair.

CHAPTER TEN

WHAT
FORGIVENESS
DOES NOT
LOOK LIKE

WHAT FORGIVENESS DOES NOT LOOK LIKE

By now we have seen that forgiveness is multidimensional.

- It is a vehicle through which grace is offered and received.
- It is God's method of rescuing humanity.
- It is an exit route from "StuckVille."
- It is a powerful shifter.
- It is a force.
- It is intensely personal.
- It is a command.
- It is a release.
- It leaves a legacy.
- It reveals God perspectives.
- It creates positive momentum.
- It draws us into intimacy with God.

Forgiveness can literally change the landscape of our world. It is not Mary Poppins, fairy dust, or three wishes in a bottle but rather a force of our human spirit received by faith, given by grace, and energized by God himself.

Are you looking for tangible results, physical facts, restored circumstances, and miraculous transformation in others? I experienced all of these when I stirred up forgiveness as a powerful lifestyle.

Forgiveness freed me from:
- believing a lie
- being locked into the facts
- offences, violations or mistakes
- the stranglehold of the past and the prospect of life in Stuckville;

And freed me to:
- be who I was created to be
- realize my potential and fulfill my dreams
- live valued and to value others
- love and be loved
- go to the party!
- it is not denial.
- it is not pious steadfastness (or taking the high moral ground).

I think it is a natural fallback position to seriously doubt that the truth-and-God combo will be adequate to get what we want done. Sometimes, God can seem a bit soft. But if we are completely honest, we also know that the actions stemming from our resentment, hurt, or hate haven't done us much good, brought us much peace or given us much relief either!

Well, God is not too soft and neither is the response he requires of us. He is strong, sovereign, powerful, loving, but equally just and fair. Living for him is not for the faint hearted but for the courageous; for those not afraid to explore their God-sized capacity; for those who will trust in a loving God.

Forgiveness is not activated automatically.
It is not a wish, its work; it is not a magic wand, its your
will and only the brave will accept what it is not.

1. FORGIVENESS IS NOT DENIAL:

Forgiveness should never be confused with denying the facts. In chapter two, I spoke of the personal responsibility and courage it takes to face the difficult facts and ask the difficult questions. Doing so will spotlight and give voice to some neglected areas of our own soul. Examples of things that might surface could be . . . "I am so easily manipulated"; "I'm so approval driven"; "I live my life for another"; "I am so unsure of my own truth." Some unpalatable realities about our own character might surface such as "I did not know I could hate like this"; "I will not be happy until they suffer as I have suffered"; "I have driven friends away but I have been so wronged."

Then we are left with some decisions:

- Do we fuel the fire or put it out?
- Do we hate or heal?
- Do we release or resent?
- Do we fight indefinitely or forgive taking an exit route for our fresh start?

No matter how we answer those questions, one thing is certain. Denial is not an option.

Denial takes no personal responsibility.
It's weak and passive stance makes no positive or
progressive steps forward and its hushed voice
sings no songs of freedom over our life.

At best, fueled by our own sense of self-fulfillment or survival, we may land ourselves a victory or two or get our own way or see some justice that aligns with our stringent requirements. We may end up with a financial benefit, a public confession, or exoneration.

I am not advocating the forfeit of rightful compensation where appropriate nor a weak and passive stance on justice or righting wrongs but all decisions need to be weighed in light of the future we desire and the person we desire to be.

Denial buries legitimate hurts alive. For a season, they may lay buried underground and silenced. But like a seed that is buried deep beneath the soil, given the right conditions, those hurts will be energized to break open the surface and spring forth, having already taken root. They will be ready to branch out and bear fruit. Rather than going away, our legitimate hurts will have taken on their own life, fed by our growing concerns, and growing resentment.

Facing the truth takes guts but truth brings the conviction necessary for change.

Change will produce the optimal outcome both for ourselves and for others in our life. But the change we most need happens firstly within our own heart. While we long to see outward change, it will come as a result of the transformation from inside us first.

Whenever Jesus contradicted the religious leaders of his day, it was to show them a higher truth. Here was one such confrontation.

"We're familiar with the old written law, "Love our friend" and its unwritten companion, "Hate your enemy." I'm challenging that. I'm telling you to love your enemies. Let them bring out the best in you, not the worst. When someone gives you a hard time, respond with the energies of prayer, for then you are working out of your true selves, your God created selves . . . If all we do is love the lovable, do we expect a bonus? Anybody can do that. If we simply say hello to those who greet us, do we expect a medal? . . . In a word, what I am saying is grow up. You're kingdom subjects. Now live like it. Live out your God-created identity. Live generously and graciously toward others, the way God lives toward you." Matthew 5:4348 (Message Bible Translation)

Confrontation forces us to make a decision. I will or I will not. I agree or I do not. I am open or I am closed. I will trust or I will be self-sufficient.

> *Where change is necessary,*
> *it is actually destructive not to change.*

For example, if we need to change our staff, it is destructive for our business not to do so. If we need to take time for our family, it is destructive not to do so. If we need to broaden our circle of friends, it is destructive not to do so. If we need to alter our eating habits, it is destructive not to do so. If our kids need to be disciplined, it is destructive not to do so, and if we need to forgive someone, it is destructive not to do so.

Ignoring offenses can be a temporary solution if we really want to avoid conflict or remain indifferent to the truth. But denial does not cause change in lives or bring solutions to circumstances. And we have already seen what indifference does! In fact, denial is a false sense of security that becomes the enemy of change.

If you are a peacemaker by nature, you may be living in denial right now—shutting away feelings, offenses and hurts; turning a blind eye to what niggles at your conscience or covering up, passing over and pushing down past opportunities that would require you to face the truth and make a decision.

Perhaps you are clinging desperately to a hope that it will all blow over or that time will heal all offenses and hurts and miraculously change you as a person. But time carries no power to heal only opportunities to do so. I had to learn this for myself as you will also. Perhaps the pain that facing the truth demands is too cruel for you as it gives voice to events that you did not want, did not deserve and cannot change.

For me, confronting the truth meant taking my head out of the sand in the temporary and safe world of denial. With this decision came the most excruciating pain requiring the most courageous decisions I have ever had to make.

I discovered that the most difficult thing to do is to break a cycle. It wasn't that hard to keep enduring or to keep going. I had learned over many years how to do that. The really hard part came when I began to put a stop to a negative cycle.

Facing the truth meant facing the giants of my circumstances and my pride. These giants were all well armed with weapons of raw reality, rejection, humiliation and belittling; and with each wound I bled my identity and self-worth. I can still hear myself saying, "This is what I get for doing what I know is right!"

For months, it seemed like I was on the front line of the battlefield and I didn't know how long I could bear the injuries. I became a walking case of information overload. The facts were cruel and the truth hurt!

This is where the rubber of forgiveness hits the road of reality.

During the nightmare of legal requirements necessary for divorce, I had to stand up for the best interests of my children and to adequately transition from Mrs. to Ms. It was a sad, mentally taxing and emotionally wounding time. Although I didn't always roll over and play dead or fully turn the other cheek, I was not interested in living in a system of weights and balances, efforts and pay backs. Nothing will ever satisfy our mind if we choose that course—no amount of change, compensation, or grace will ever be enough from another. We will always require more. We will always feel cheated.

The truth I was about to face really hurt, but not as much (I suspected) as the truth I would always wonder about.

So I took responsibility for facing the details of truth. I looked the enemy of reality and information in the face—the starkness of what had happened to my world, to my life, to my marriage, and why. In so doing, I faced the unknown which was lying behind the curtain of my future.

The truth about who I had become caused me to see myself as though I was an observer peering through the glass panes of my own life. I wept for her with the brave heart but the tired mind. I wept for her with the capable exterior and the fragile will. I wept for the broken vase, the broken dreams and the broken heart.

And then it was time to stop! It was time to nurture my famished and weak soul. So here's what I did . . . I took solace and comfort in the presence of good friends and family visits. I ate chocolate, drank good coffee, and good wine and made retail therapy my new life coach!

I was through the season of survival and now it was my season to live! I was going to the party!

No, forgiveness is definitely not denial. Quite the opposite. It faces the truth, makes a decision, and requires dedication. Accompanying dedication is discipline (or the rearranging of life to line up with where we want it to go). Such discipline may be to recognize responses and behavior patterns that need adjusting and then set about implementing the changes.

2. FORGIVENESS IS NOT A PIOUS STEADFASTNESS (or taking the high moral ground)

Forgiveness should also not be confused with a passive resolve to wait out the problem. There is nothing noble or righteous about "putting up with it." If we self-righteously confuse forgiveness with "love endures all things" (you know, the verses read out at weddings) then we will have mistaken love for weakness and forgiveness for self-righteousness.

The enduring nature of love is seen in its victory over adversity; its power in the face of hatred; its expansion despite restricting circumstances and its light that illuminates and causes change in dark places. No, love doesn't put up with; love conquers, invades, and wins! It is the character and nature of God in us—it cannot lose!

The danger of a "just put up with it" mentality is that our passive resolve to do nothing will perhaps perpetuate an offender's actions. A no comment or a no vote can be taken as passive agreement. In other words, our no show, no stand, no opinion says we are okay with the offense continuing. If we are the subject of the offense, it will continue. If we are the observer of an offense, we give permission. If we are the offender, we dull our conscience for lack of conviction to change. Not to act is not an option.

The eighteenth century Irish political philosopher, Edmund Burke, famously said that for evil to triumph, all it takes is for good people to do nothing.

Forgiveness is not the old English "stiff upper lip" or teeth-gritting determination to keep going no matter what. Neither is it a macabre sort of humility. Forgiveness is the child of love and an ally of faith carrying with it the grace force to enable us not to put up with but to see things through with strength in every circumstance in our life. Forgivenesss means we can do all of this while retaining our dignity, refining our vision, and renewing our thinking.

CHAPTER ELEVEN

WHAT FORGIVENESS DOES

WHAT FORGIVENESS DOES

In this next chapter, I want to be practical about what to expect from forgiveness for ourselves and for others and what to expect concerning the impact it will have in our world.

1. FORGIVENESS RELEASES OTHERS:

Hold tight. Whenever there is grace or allowances for the unlovely and unlikely in our world, the spin off always touches and enhances ours. Releasing others is the first step toward our freedom!

Unlike tolerance which makes allowances for petty annoyances and personal preferences; forgiveness grants the free pardon of a legitimate debt owed and gives up all claim to it and reference to it.

Stop for a moment and try to imagine what that does for another who is guilty of a crime or offense. Maybe this is so distasteful for you right now that it seems too inhumane to go there. But the most humane thing we can do, not just for another, but for ourselves, is to dig deep for the courage to go there.

To forgive or to pardon is not saying that the one who hurts us was right. But it is saying that we trust God with the outcomes when WE do what is right. Nor is it saying that the one who hurt us has to become our best buddy or that we must "do coffee." We may choose never to have contact with that one again. It is our choice.

A friend of mine experienced the turnabout power of forgiveness when he literally released someone from a debt owed to his family. This story is not a formula to instruct us but rather an amazing illustration of the depth and penetrable dimensions of this gift.

It was normally a quiet suburban street where kids rode their scooters, bikes, and skateboards. But this day, a well-known biker group came riding in with revenge on their minds. Speed was part and parcel of their image and local laws were their hatred not their hindrance.

In an untimely event, my friend's little girl ran across the road to join the other neighborhood kids who had gathered to play. She was hit by one of the bikers and thrown into the air landing on the opposite side of the street. In what we can only call a miracle, she lives and walks today but suffered several broken bones and still today wears the facial scars inflicted by bitumen and bike.

His daughter was still in hospital when my friend visited the jail where the guilty biker was kept until trial and pending bail. The group and any individual associated with them were under the suspicious eye of police and gladly apprehended for any misdemeanors. Bail was set for several thousand dollars but loyalty among them soon became defined when no one from his biker "family" came forward.

My friend, in a surprising act of grace, paid the bail price, and the undeserving culprit walked out free and forgiven. The events that followed are neither a formula nor a guarantee but nevertheless, one of those uncommon results that stem from uncommon actions. The biker insisted on speaking to my friend and so they arranged to meet. He was anxious to know why. "Why would the father not want revenge?"; "Why would the father pay his bail?"; "Why was the father not angry?" The truth is, my friend did get angry, he instinctively wanted revenge and could have used the money in a million different ways for his own family. But he chose forgiveness and he explained it in the only way he knew how.

He told the story of a loving God who gave his only son to pay the price for his own debts. While still undeserving and unchanged, Jesus paid a price that he could never afford, released him from a debt that he would not hold against him and stands even today on his behalf as his lawyer and advocate before the great judge—his Father God.

The tattooed, weight lifting hulk of a man could only turn his head away in shame as the tears made their tracks down his weather beaten face. For perhaps the first time, the curtain was drawn back revealing grace at its finest and the overwhelming response that followed can only be attributed to the power of love demonstrated that day through a work of forgiveness.

The little girl was never told how the big man who became known as uncle came into their lives. But he was there at every birthday and a place setting laid at each family or festive event. He was a familiar figure at every milestone in her life and, at her twenty-first birthday, she spoke of an uncle who was as close, and as formative in her growing up years as a father.

One man was released from the bitter tentacles of revenge and unforgiveness. One man was given the occasion to respond to grace. One man did.

The result? Many were blessed. Lives were directed away from the roadblock and no one ended up in Stuckville for very long.

With racism being an incubator for wretchedly cruel behavior, the words of Martin Luther King, Jr. take on great relevance. He said, *Somehow we must be able to stand up before our most bitter opponents and say: "We shall match your capacity to inflict suffering by our capacity to endure suffering. We will meet your physical force with soul force. Do to us what you will and we will still love you . . . But be assured that we'll wear you down by our capacity to suffer, and one day we will win our freedom. We will not only win freedom for ourselves; we will so appeal to your heart and conscience that we will win you in the process, and our victory will be a double victory."*
[Extract from a Christmas Sermon on Peace delivered by Martin Luther King. JR. 1967]

2. FORGIVENESS RELEASES US:

*It's natural to want mercy for ourselves
but judgment for others. It's because we judge
others by their actions but we judge
ourselves by our intentions.*

Perhaps the most difficult action required of forgiveness is the first one. In other words, to be the one who initiates it. Jesus gave illustrations that suggest there is no differentiation between the one who has been offended and the offendee—he was speaking to both.[26]

*As stinging as this may be if we happen to be
the one offended, our hunger to move on must outweigh
our desire to hang on.*

There is something about the effects of a closed heart. Where there is a refusal to offer grace in one area, this one closed door sets a precedent of closed doors in other areas of life until eventually we become imprisoned in a self-imposed asylum of justification.

It becomes easy to behave very poorly because we can always justify, explain, and reason away our reactions, feelings, and responses.

Yes, we hold the key to the change that we desire in the people, circumstances, and world around us. It always begins with us. Forgiveness can release the true sweetness and strength of our personality and it can uncover and reveal it in others.

*Our actions will always locate our
heart and our words will always publish
what's in our heart.*

Some of our friends will benefit from siding with us, others will experience the fall out of our coldness, and still others will see through us and be repelled. Whether we choose to forgive or to hold onto our pious steadfastness, we are managing the relationship dynamics through our mood, we are creating the boarders of our life by our attitude, and we are forming our future by our words and actions.

LETTING IT GO

There is an ancient story entitled The Unforgiving Servant that disarmingly reveals how we so quickly seek forgiveness for ourselves but so easily hold on to the offences of others.[27] The story goes like this:

A king decided to square accounts with his servants. However, one servant that was brought before him had run up a debt of about one hundred thousand dollars. He couldn't pay up. So as was the legal right and custom of the day, the king ordered that the man, his wife, his children, and all his goods be sold off at the slave market.

The poor wretch threw himself at the king's feet and begged the king to give him a chance and some time and he would pay it all back. The king was so touched by the plea that he let him off and erased the debt.

The servant was no sooner out of the room when he came upon one of his own fellow servants who happened to owe him ten dollars. He seized him by the throat and demanded he pay up now!

The poor wretch threw himself down and begged for a chance and some time and he would pay it all back. But he wouldn't do it. The ungrateful servant had the man arrested and put into jail until the debt was paid in full.

When the other servants saw what was going on, they were outraged and brought a detailed report to the king.

The king summoned the man and told him how disgusted he was. "I forgave your whole debt, as large as it was, when you begged for mercy. Shouldn't you be compelled to be merciful to your fellow servants who also ask for mercy?"

The king was furious and put the screws to the man until he paid back the entire debt.

This story was told to answer the question, "How many times must I forgive someone who has hurt me?" The answer was clear. It's on going. It's a lifestyle we cultivate to safeguard against imprisoning ourselves in a self-imposed asylum of justification.

> *"Forgiveness is not an occasional act;*
> *it is a permanent attitude."*
> Martin Luther King

It's too easy not to forgive; it takes very little effort to conjure up thoughts and actions of malice, revenge, and self-gratification. But somehow, unforgiveness backfires.

Unforgiveness will torment our mind and keep us tied to events that roadblock us, diminish our view of the path ahead, disguise the picture of our own capacity, and dim the light on what an energized us looks like. We will expend so much energy concerned with what is owed us that we will have very little left to expand our own capacity and really enjoy what we have.

My mother told me a story of a little boy and his sister visiting their grandparents on their farm. One afternoon, the boy took his grandpa's rifle and began to practice his shooting skills with cans lined up against the back fence. He mostly missed every can but he accidentally shot the duck! He hid the duck as far down the property as he could drag it and then returned the rifle. As he made his way back to the house, his sister called out, "I saw what you did and I won't tell if you do what I say!"

That night at dinner, grandma asked who would help wash up the dishes. "Paul will as I have a letter to write," replied the girl. Then she whispered to him, "Remember the duck?" The next morning, grandpa asked who would like to go fishing with him and who would like to stay home and help grandma. The girl replied, "Paul said he will help grandma so I will go with you." Then she whispered to him, "Remember the duck?"

This went on for the rest of the week until the boy could no longer stand it or live with the guilt. He approached his grandma and told her that he had accidentally shot their duck and that his sister knew about it. The kind grandma replied, "Yes I know son, I saw it happen. I was just interested in how long you would let your sister control and hold you captive."

Living in a system of trying to balance weights and scales is a narrow and steely existence. Others will never measure up and we will always operate at a loss.

We have not been seized and locked up by God until we could pay up for the miserable effort we call life. Quite the opposite. We have been released and pardoned from all prior convictions and more than that—the provision of forgiveness extends beyond the "now" barrier to encompass our future too! Our valuable and purpose-filled life has been spring-boarded beyond the grasp of the past and into the grip of a grace-filled future!

To experience the release that someone else' actions have had over us is to see the supernatural touch the natural. It is to know we have removed the roadblocks that hinder our friendship with God. It is beginning to see others as God sees them. It is to free and uncomplicate our journey. It is to be convinced that there is no better highway to be on.

And we can pray from our heart the prayer, "Father forgive me my debts as I forgive my debtors."[28]

WHAT FORGIVENESS DOES NOT DO

— CHAPTER TWELVE —

WHAT FORGIVENESS DOES NOT DO

1. FORGIVENESS DOES NOTWORK LIKE ATEST TUBE FORMULA:

This life is not about "If I do this, God will do that." In fact, God is under no obligation to perform for us like our fairy godfather and he doesn't exist to grant us our every desire. However, the anicent poet, King David, wrote: *Delight yourself in the Lord (willingly choose His higher perspectives) and He shall give you the desires of your heart. Psalm 37:4 The Lord will give grace and glory, no good thing will He withhold from those who walk uprightly (those who choose to defy gravity in their thinking) (my brackets added). Psalm 84:11b*

Have I just contradicted myself? No. Although God is not a fairy godfather, he loves us personally and when we trust in God's character, we tap into God's life-giving principles which give us an over-the-top life instead of being stuck in our old habitual patterns of being and doing.

I read an article once in a marketing strategy magazine. It told of a well-known packet cake mix brand. The manufacturers had changed their formula to simplify the cake-making process even further. The cake mix no longer required eggs and oil to be added, only water. The sales of the popular brand plummeted to an all time low.

Research into public opinion revealed that most people preferred to feel as though they had a "hand" in the process and that adding the extra ingredients helped them achieve that feeling of ownership and credit. So the recipe was reconstructed to again require oil and eggs and of course, sales went up!

There will be times when we feel we need to "have a hand" in the process of forgiveness to feel like our vital ingredients will complete the formula of our happy ever after picture. That it is *our responsibility* to make them aware of their error! That it is our duty to inform others what really happened. That it is our right to make it hard for them. That it is our prerogative to insist they pay up!

But the work of forgiveness is not a test tube formula where a sterile controlled environment and the right amount of chemicals are mixed in an isolated container and left to stand for a prescribed time to produce the results needed for every situation. It doesn't work that way and it doesn't actually need the addition of our oil and eggs. In fact, mostly our "oil and eggs" just complicate and draw out the process. It's God's cake mix and he knows what ingredients are needed. So add the water, or, decision to release a legitimate debt, and give God permission to do what we cannot.

Forgiveness is not a quick-fix formula for a happy ever after picture. It's not an attitude that we put on today to get a result that we want and take off tomorrow depending on the circumstances and how we feel. It's a lifestyle that becomes us and it is lived out in the dirt, the pain, and the raw reality of life consistently.

Every unique situation will require releasing a legitimate debt but every unique situation will also require thoughtful responses, patience, and a peaceful resolve that we will find our healing with time.

We can hate that it takes time. We might hate that there are times of personal responsibility where we are required to retrain our minds and hands to act differently. And we can resent the feelings of powerlessness that come with a "hands off" approach to those who have hurt us. But this is where a life of forgiveness comes into its own. Like a pebble touching the waters of your heart, the ripples begin to move out from you in a never-ending gentle but consistent stream. Not surprising then, those around you are touched and never quite the same either. We begin living a life of trust assuring us that God knows the end of our life's picture from the beginning and that his plans for us are for good and not evil.[29] The work of forgiveness is complete. So when we offer it to another in a true act of grace, we do not need to add to it or do God's work for him—it is complete. To arrive at this place sees us beginning to redirect our internal energy to external areas that actually stretch us and expand our capacity and boarders rather than restrict them. A friend once said to me, "When you get consumed with your own problems, find someone else in need and become a solution to theirs. You will not only feel better, you'll get better."

When I was desperate for quick fixes and immediate solutions, when I thought that doing my best now meant that I would get what I deserved now, I took my friend's advice. I remained involved in leading a small life-coaching group and found a role in a church-based charity Christmas concert. Self conceived formulas of what I thought I deserved began to fall away as I invested some of the energy from my pain and problems into the lives of others. I began to heal me. I didn't realize it at the time but I was becoming the future I desired.

2.   FORGIVENESS DOES NOT GUARANTEE OUR "HAPPY EVER AFTER" PICTURE:

Our "heaven on earth" may not happen overnight. In fact, our pictures of heaven on earth may not happen at all. Are you prepared for that?

Unfortunately, unless we live on an island isolated from other human beings, we will encounter people who think differently to us; people who make different choices; people who have different values and standards to us. Some of these people will have influence in our life and impact our world directly or indirectly to varying degrees. You may be at a place right now, a place you never intended to be, partly as a result of decisions others made.

I have been in that place.

I began to consciously remind myself that all people have their own free will; and all free wills have been filtered through personal experiences of parenting, role modeling, relationships, and resulting views of God and the world.

Then I reminded myself that I, too, had a free will! Remember, people can only affect us (and some will do so with their hate or imprisoning opinions) if we allow them to. And so, through forgiveness, I found a strength that produced the fruit of strength. I found courage that produced the fruit of courage. And I found trust that produced the fruit of trust.

With or without my happily-ever-after, forgiveness was adding luster to my days. I was no longer at the complete mercy of those with whom I felt misaligned.

Perhaps for you extending forgiveness has a string attached to it. Perhaps you are expectant for the return of a child, a spouse, or a friend. Perhaps you are desperate for reconciliation, an apology, justice, compensation, or acquittal. But by trusting in God's love and grace, you will reach a moment in time where you can say, "I trust God to paint the picture of my happy ever after," and leave the brush strokes to him.

My happily-ever-after . . .

I began the first year of my seven years alone checking on my foundation.

Remember, trusting God with the outcomes of our life is not a passive resolve of wait and see but more like rowing a boat—building strength and momentum by paddling toward calm waters or the other side of the lake whilst building wisdom by paddling away from the rocks!

Redefining life as I wanted it to look could not be shaky, indecisive, led by emotion or determined by circumstances, and other people. It had to be more solid than that, more reliable, and long term.

> *No one can reach their dreams*
> *if they think their circumstances, other people*
> *or events control their life.*

I wanted my foundation to stand the test of time and storm. Over the next few years, I began to strategically work God's foundational words into my life. What he said about me was what I said about me. What he thought about me was what I thought about me. Where the Bible talked about someone being blessed, restored, set apart, elevated, promoted, or loved, I underlined it and inserted my name! Wherever there was an occasion to win, use wisdom, know truth, gain experience or lead, I underlined it and inserted my name! Presumptuous? Maybe. Expectant? Absolutely!

. . . Was even happier than happily-ever-after.

In the first year as a single mum, I also began to build. I worked three jobs for six months then I retrained to enter the world of dentistry again. Five years later, I really began to live the dream and traded clinic for lectern. For seven years, I raised my sons, raised my sights, and raised my expectations.

My original "happy-ever-after" picture could not be recreated and I learned to live in the realm of expectant faith believing that God had something even greater for me.

On one recent morning, I was driving down the highway when I noticed a rather large billboard displaying the words, "Expect a Miracle." Where this type of billboard would normally be advertising motor vehicles, insurance packages or real estate, on this day it was advertising the availability of miracles!

I don't need a miracle every day and I know that my expectations don't make God feel obliged to perform. But something happens on the inside at the deepest levels when I begin to expect that my life will be marked by miracles or blessing (things that happen when God is working on my behalf). It doesn't mean that every day forward will be perfect and that I will get everything I'm wishing for. But the very idea of expecting a miracle opened my eyes and heart to see what I would have missed before.

What does expectancy look like? It looks like an open hand, open eyes, an open door, an open heart, and an open mind—all ready to receive.

Our beloved boarder collie has done this whole journey with us and is now quite old in dog years. As an elderly citizen, we have afforded him privileges few dogs live to enjoy. One of the nightly routines is his wander outside before settling in to his fur rug on our study floor—a place he chose where he gets the full view of the running of the household. He is expectant that each night I will have a dog treat for him. Before he sees it, before I even make a move to get it, he begins the four-step dance from one foot to another. With tail wagging, feet dancing, and tongue licking in expectancy, he knows I'll produce the treat. Why? I always do. He never shies away, retreats tail between legs, or cowers into a corner. Why? He knows that kindness is what he can expect from us. We love him.

I have learnt that it is similar to expecting God's goodness, kindness, consistency, and love; to wait expectantly for his generous father provision. This stance of expectancy will have our life looking forward rather than backward, prepared, ready and making room for God to move on our behalf; ready for the inevitable change in the landscape of our relationships and circumstances. Our life's posture will be ready for life's opportunities. I can't express this more accurately than the ancient writings which say:

The fundamental fact of existence is that this trust in God, this faith, is the firm foundation under everything that makes life worth living. It's our handle on what we can't see. Hebrews 11:1 Message Bible translation.

I have been told that, during the healing process, bones become stronger in places that were fractured or broken. It is the same for broken hearts. And just as the cut of a surgeon's knife can bring immense good, even to the saving of life—so can God create good out of bad. God is wiser than any skilled microsurgeon working deep inside the intricate cellular walls of our heart.

The best surgeons boast of minimal scarring. Trust what you will look like to God. And trust that a stronger, healthier you will create something strangely and beautifully different in your world than what you knew before.

WHO DO WE FORGIVE?

— CHAPTER THIRTEEN —

WHO DO WE FORGIVE?

Unfortunately, one thing is sure when we live on planet earth; people may desert us, hate us, lie to us, leave us, deceive us, cheat on us, divorce us, use us, abuse us, speak ill of us, abandon us, ignore us, or try to control us—but God never will. And even if we have trouble believing a word of it, he still believes in us. He still believes in our capacity to repay evil with good. He still believes that the force of grace is as active in us as it is within him.

Forgiveness is not an occasional act or nor is it confined to the "Christian thing to do." Rather, it is a permanent attitude that forges life forward.

- It's the way we choose to respond over reacting.
- It's the way we choose to retain our dignity in the face of injustice.
- It's the way we choose to reply when slandered or degraded.
- It's how we choose who our friends are after a betrayal.
- It's where we choose to position ourselves when the chips are down.
- It's how we speak of the future after a crisis.
- It's the legacy we leave behind us in the midst of tragedy.

It may be that the recipient who most needs our grace gift is the one most unlikely or least thought of in our world. This is not to say that we are to go on a witch hunt through memory lane trying to draw out possible candidates, but it is a reminder that our mind is a manic collector of our experiences and that our subconscious mind is a warehouse storing them up.

This is our software for filtering information, making decisions, and responding to the world around us.

In recalling past habits and patterns, we will most likely cringe at how we responded to certain people or situations in our world.

1. FORGIVE OURSELVES:

Sometimes, the roadblock starts and finishes with us. Whether we have been offended or offended someone else, we deserve forgiveness. Whether we think we are a good person or one who is unworthy, we need and deserve forgiveness. It's time to give yourself that gift.

If God considers us worthy of forgiveness, then who are we to argue with him? He sent his only son as a gift to all people guilty and undeserving. The force of that gift has changed lives, influenced cultures, ended slavery, intercepted racism, and propagated his outrageous love to humanity for thousands of years. Are we going to argue that point with God? If he says we are worthy, then we are!

Hurt hearts often become guarded and barricaded and often end up as bitter spirits. I neither understood nor knew how important it was to extend grace, love and forgiveness to myself until I arrived at that place where I knew I needed a fresh start.

After the divorce, my soul was left bankrupt and my tank empty. Behind me were too many withdrawals and not enough deposits. I faced a choice to either gird myself and reinforce myself with layers of self-protection and self-sufficiency, or expose myself for what I really was—grieving and emotionally undernourished.

My sense of failure as a wife, a mother, a daughter, a sister, a leader, and a friend took me to regretful places in my past. I knew the only way forward was to go back. So I went back and I gave myself the gift of grace. I forgave me:

- for not being able to fulfill the dream picture
- for letting go
- for hanging on
- for covering up
- for being tough
- for being soft

- for submitting
- for controlling
- for being controlled
- for believing anything
- for trusting blindly
- for not trusting my intuition
- for not seeing
- for making tough decisions
- for living up to my name
- for not living up to my name
- for not listening
- for shifting blame
- for letting us down
- for being the only me I knew to be at the time

So as fascinated as I am with forward, I realized that the process of forgiving myself would require me to travel back for a little while in order to travel forward.

Perhaps the most difficult decision you will make is to travel back to the place where you failed, got hurt or hurt someone else. For most people, dreams and visions have already been forsaken and a common response is to just go back to the familiar. The disciple Peter did.

After the death of Jesus, Peter's dreams were shattered. This fisherman had encountered the messiah. In him he had found a friend and mentor. In him he had found value without judgment. In him he had found God without religion. Full of the pain of recent loss, disillusioned, and disappointed, we find Peter back at the docks. His boat however, did not offer the same sense of destiny that hours on foot with Jesus did. Talk of weather, markets, and trade prices did not evoke his passion to things eternal nor stir his capacity for greater than the mundane. Days at sea could not erase his memories of the one who touched his heart and changed his life. But monumentally more, they couldn't block out the night Jesus was arrested and Peter, through fear of the crowd, denied having even known him—not once, or even twice, but three times.

But it's right here on the sea and in the fishing trawler that Peter's thoughts are interrupted by a voice from the shore. "Catch anything?" Probably just a peasant hoping for a handout.

But John is with Peter and he knows that voice! Peter's instant impulse is to lunge over board and swim to shore. Dripping wet as he stood before Jesus, Peter perhaps for the first time in his life is lost for words.

Jesus had made a small fire and begun breakfast for his friends. Silence. The last time Peter stood by a fire—Peter had failed. He stood before Jesus too shameful and broken for words but too expectant to leave. But God had come. This moment is precious and it is personal. Jesus was offering more than breakfast to the friend who had betrayed him—He was offering grace—and through it, Peter found himself forgiven.[30]

Forgiveness undeserved and unearned cuts the cords of guilt and lets the burden of it roll away. History does not record Peter as the fickle one who betrayed the son of God; not at all. On the backs of such transformed lives, Christ built his church! Peter was about the poorest choice Jesus could have made for building his community of faith; but that could be why Jesus started with him—so that you and I would not disqualify ourselves. If Peter was found worthy, forgiven, loved, and fit as a role model for the church and family of God, then there is also a place where we fit.

**Principle—One of the most difficult decisions
I will make is to travel back to the place where
I failed, got hurt or hurt someone else.
Going back can be the starting place for a
fresh beginning.**

- I choose to travel back where necessary.
- If I need to receive forgiveness for mistakes I have made, I will stand repentant, amazed, and grateful before God.
- I accept the value, the significance, the forgiveness, and love he offers me.
- I choose to take him up on his offer of a fresh start with him.

2. **FORGIVE GOD**

Let me begin by saying that the bad things that happen to us do not have a meaning when they happen to us. For instance, there was no meaning to the senseless accident which threw my friend's little girl across the road. However, we can redeem tragedies from being merely senseless by giving meaning to them. In so doing, we replace the old "Why did this have to happen?" question with the "What am I going to do now that this has happened?" question.

The notion of forgiving God may strike a painful chord with us if we have ever asked, "How could a loving God allow that to happen?" or the idea of forgiving him may sound offensive to us because, although we have been hurt, we have believed in a perfect, loving, and just God. Either way, unconscious confusion and blame can build up against God and it will subtly outwork itself as doubt, arrogance, and eventual distance.

The loss of a child, the unfaithful spouse, the financial crisis, the physical abuse, the handicaps and unfulfilled dreams will have even the most faith-filled person pulling God out of the humanly crafted box he has put him in and demanding he give an account!

I believe in God but I do not believe all the same things about him that I believed while growing up. I recognize that he has gifted us with the laws of the universe and with human moral freedom and choice. I don't hold God responsible for accidents, sickness, and natural disasters because I realize that we live on a fragile planet which has been polluted morally and environmentally by humankinds' poor management and I also realize that I have little to gain and much to lose when I blame God for those things.

I can believe in and love a God who hates suffering but cannot eliminate it all, far more easily than I can love a God who chooses to make children starve and people suffer and die for whatever exalted reason. For those who think differently, I would say, "My God is not cruel, sorry about yours."

I now see life and all its events a bit like a game of football. Although I grew up with Aussie Rules football in Victoria (the game of champions), and then moved to Queensland where Rugby dominates weekend TV and sports grounds ("catch me kill me"), I can't say that I fully have a handle on either game's rules. However, I was fascinated to learn a little about the rules of American football. ("Pad me up and knock me over")

I now know that the quarterback is the main man. He's the one who throws the ball. The game is all about statistics—how far he throws and how many complete passes he makes. A complete pass is when the catcher actually catches the ball. But sometimes he might be out of position and the ball might hit him in the chest or he might fumble the ball and drop it. Then it is called an incomplete pass and the quarterback's stats go down—even though it may have been a fantastic pass by the quarterback!

When people drop the ball (when children go hungry, women are raped, men are undervalued, minorities are marginalized, cities are bombed . . .), then there has been an incomplete pass and God's stats go down! His pass was perfect, the ball was sufficient, and the aim was accurate but his stats are affected by our poor positioning and he wears the blame.

God doesn't cause our misfortunes. Some are caused by bad timing, some by bad people, and some by bad choices. The painful things that happen to us are not punishments for our mistakes or misbehaviors, nor are they in anyway a part of some grand design sent from God. Because the tragedy is not God's will, we need never feel betrayed, abandoned, or hurt by him. To help us overcome it, we remind ourselves that "God is as outraged by it as we are."

If that is the case, we may be asking, "If God didn't cause it and he doesn't prevent it, what use is God then and why should I turn to him?"

First of all, God has created a world in which many more good things than bad things happen. Tragedy and disaster affect us not just because they are painful but because they are the exception. Most mornings, I wake up feeling good. Any illness I have had has been curable. I have lived in the same house for four years and never been robbed. I have shopped at the same shopping malls and never been mugged. I've driven the same motorways and never had an accident. My children have always returned home safely.

The inoperable tumor, the abduction, the robbery, the cyclone are all life-shattering exceptions. They are rarer than the normal goodness in our days. When we have been hurt or swept up in an "exception," then this is a hard pill to swallow. It becomes a large object and, when we are standing very close to a large object, all we can see is the bigness of that object. Only as we step back can we see its dimensions and the landscape around it.

When we have been stunned by one of life's exceptions, we can only see and feel the tragedy. It will take time and distance to see it in the context of our life, the lives around us, and the world at whole.

In the Jewish tradition, there is a prayer known as the Mourners' Kaddish. It is not about death but about life and it praises God for creating a good and livable and friendly world. As the mourner recites it, he is reminded of all that is good and worth living for. There is great benefit in keeping our mind on what has enriched, or can enrich us, rather than only on our loss.

So how does God make a difference in our lives? Here is just one magnificent way.

God has placed within our DNA an inspired urge for people to help people. By coming along side, both professionally trained and ordinary people alike help, comfort, and protect others from danger, from being alone, feeling abandoned, being judged. Such people sustain life and alleviate pain.

God helps by inspiring people to help people. God shows his opposition to these exceptions by summoning friends, neighbors, business people, trades people, councils, governments, pastors, and families to ease the burdens and fill the gaps.

When I was alone with no money and very few options, I was sustained by family, friends, and others who made a point of showing they cared and understood. When I was diagnosed with a potential life threatening illness, they journeyed with me. By their presence in my life, I was resourced, encouraged and coached to redefine my life. They inspired me to move forward and live gratefully.

Have you experienced God's hands in your life through someone in your world? And can you see that you were Jesus with skin on to someone in your world?

Then there are the times when, without people, God declares himself in ways that have involved no human hands. We call these ways "miracles."

Are you capable of forgiving and accepting a world which has disappointed you by not being perfect; a world in which there is so much disunity, cruelty, unfairness, disease, crime, and random tragedy? Can you forgive its imperfections and love it simply because it also contains great beauty and goodness and because right now, it's the only world we have?

Principle—Because tragedy is not God's will, I need never feel betrayed, abandoned or hurt by him. I remind myself that God is as outraged by misfortune as I am.

- I see where I have shifted blame and put it on God.
- I recognize the fact of "an incomplete pass" in my life . . . a time when I or someone in my world was not positioned well for the game and the ball was dropped.
- Within the context of what I now understand, I forgive God . . . or at least my mistaken understanding of him.

---

3. FORGIVE FAMILY

Someone once said to me that parents are just kids who grew up and had kids. Wisdom sometimes comes with age and sometimes age just comes alone! Sometimes we don't learn . . . we just grow up.

I doubt if there be a child who has ever lived who did not find an occasion to forgive their parents; and equally, a parent who has not had reason to forgive a child.

Unfortunately, families do not give immunity to hurt and betrayal and it is often in this very place where we should find solace, protection, unity, love, and support that the darkest secrets reside and the most debilitating patterns emerge.

A mother yells to her son, "I never want to see you again!" And she gets her wish, suffers from it every day and feels the pain every time she hears his name.

Siblings who shared their childhood together and almost the same genetic code can't sit in the same room together.

Husbands and wives who pledged their love and commitment to each other squeeze each other out of assets from a distance. Every night he waits for her to approach him but she never does. Each night she waits for him to come to her but he never does. Each one perpetuates the cycle. Neither will forgive.

We cannot go back and change the past, repaint the picture or retell the story but we can choose to use different brush strokes to redefine our life's landscape and thereby leave a different legacy for those who will follow us.

Families are often plagued with the same generational choices. These are not curses but choices. The son is an alcoholic just like his father. The daughter is manipulative just like her mother. The kids are prejudiced just like the parents.

If this resonates with you; if you have been influenced, infected, and incorporated, you still have your greatest and most powerful asset—your own free will and choice.

In families, forgiveness alone can halt the cycle of blaming and feuding, breaking the chain of "ungrace." Of course we will think of the hundred and one good reasons why we shouldn't forgive: "She needs to learn a lesson." "He needs to learn responsible behavior." "She needs to know how it feels." "He needs to know that his actions have consequences." "I was wronged so it's not up to me to make the first step." "Why should I forgive if they are not even sorry?"

All of a sudden, Hinduism with its doctrine of karma seems far more attractive and in line with our sense of "fairness."

Hindu scholars have calculated with mathematical precision how long it may take for one person's justice to be worked out. For punishment to balance out a person's wrongs in his life and future lives, 6,800,000 incarnations would be needed. And something in us agrees, "Yeah, now that's payback!"

In the New Testament, the most common Greek word for "forgiveness" means "to hurl away, to release and free ourselves."

Passing blame, wearing attitudes, living resentment, and holding grudges can bleat its inane dialogue through days, weeks, months, years, and even generations until one person says, "Stop! I'll break this chain. I'm sorry, will you forgive me?"

Even though forgiveness will not settle all the questions starting with "why" or all the questions of fairness, it does give a relationship a chance to start over, begin afresh.

Principle—In families, forgiveness alone can break the cycle of blaming and feuding, breaking the chain of "ungrace."

- I can retain my aloofness, hurt, anger, or resentment toward my family and so risk becoming like them, perpetuating the generational choices. Instead, I choose to offer grace, freeing my family from their emotional hold, and freeing myself from their effects.
- I take stock of any generational choices and family patterns that I am propagating. I refuse to tie any further family members up with these behaviors.
- I forgive my parents for not being as wise, strong, loving, or perfect as I needed them to be.

We can offer our family something they may never get from anyone else in the world—the gift that costs us everything, takes nothing from us and releases us to become a better and stronger person. We can forgive our family!

4. FORGIVE OTHERS: Beyond Justice

Now you know that forgiveness is not limp or weak. It does not give unjustified mercy to an offender while leaving you martyred with the consequences.

Yet, it remains that the "doing" of forgiveness can be a mystery. We are now looking at forgiving those outside of our family circle. The questions that we might ask are: "How do we forgive?"; "What does that look like for us?"; "How do we forgive people if we don't trust them?"; "How do we forgive someone who keeps breaking a promise, reoffending or doesn't ask for it?"; "Why should we forgive if we were the one wronged?"; "Must we forgive someone who has almost destroyed us?"

Many of these questions have already been answered in this book. In short, only a lifestyle of forgiveness will reward us with greater emotional health and stability as its power releases us from the grip of circumstance (the force that holds us back) and into the grip of grace (the force that carries us forward.)

The challenge comes when we have an emotional, physical or intellectual legal right to hate someone for the hurt, offense, violation, or neglect they have inflicted upon us. Jesus had such a right. Perhaps nowhere is there a more powerful yet confusing statement than that heard from Christ's most excruciating hour on the cross of crucifixion when he said, "Father forgive them, for they do not know what they are doing."[31] Instead of a cry for justice, he cried for mercy upon those who were taking his life.

History's greatest crime had just been committed.

Surrounded by jeering taunts, weakened by the loss of blood, twitching in agony with cramping muscles and dehydrating membranes, his lips are moving. "What is he saying or trying to say?"; "Is He cursing those below?"; "Is it just groans from unimaginable pain?"; "Is he delirious?" No, he is speaking words of forgiveness. "Father, forgive them." The Greek texts imply that he kept repeating the words. "Father forgive them for they do not know what they are doing."

But they DID know what they were doing. They were neither ignorant nor stupid! Judas knew he had betrayed a friend; Pilate knew he had condemned an innocent man; the religious leaders knew they had bribed false witnesses to substantiate their charges in their midnight kangaroo court; the lictor knew what he was doing with each stroke of the whip and the Roman centurions knew what they were doing as executioners when they drove the five-inch iron spike into Jesus's hands and feet. None were ignorant; all of them knew what they were doing.

We know that none were ignorant of their crime but it appears that they were ignorant of the *enormity* of their crime. The Apostle Paul later wrote, "None of the rulers of this age understood it, for if they had, they would not have crucified the Lord of glory." 1 Corinthians 2:8 (New King James Version)

Their crimes were far greater than they could have ever imagined because they did not know how far the ripples would reach, how impacting the consequences, how deep the hurt, or how sinister the plot.

Their crimes were far greater than they could have ever imagined because they failed to realize the infinite value of the person they condemned.

Those who have hurt you probably knew what they were doing too. But I am convinced that they did not understand the infinite worth and value you are to God and to our world. If they understood what God knows and thinks of you, and if they knew the depth of his love toward you, they would not have dared caused you such pain. The degree to which you find grace and courage to believe this will be proportional to the degree you can forgive and receive forgiveness.

Perhaps now his words are not so confusing. He prayed them aloud so that we could find ourselves in that prayer.

A Two-Edged Sword

Mostly, we cannot choose whether or not we suffer. We simply know that we have already suffered and that we will probably have times of suffering ahead. But we can choose not to let suffering make us bitter, revengeful, less loving, and stuck.

If we have found ourselves blaming others for the reason, we are the way we are then we have admitted that we have given others permission to control our lives. Our world reduces to survival of the fittest and we are back at the laws of the jungle.

The capacities to forgive and start afresh in our thinking and behavior are outstanding characteristics that differentiate us from the animal world. This is not just our capacity to think, but our capacity to control the way we think; to repent; to take a 180-degree turnabout in direction; to forgive; and to start a new cycle.

Many have watched a drama of forgiveness played out on the stages of the world in the musical version of Victor Hugo's novel Les Miserables. In the story Jean Valjean, a French prisoner, is hounded and then ultimately transformed by the power of forgiveness.

Jean Valjean finds himself sentenced to nineteen years of hard labor for the crime of stealing bread. Within a short time, he has turned into a hardened criminal. No one can break his will or beat him in a fight. At last, Valjean earns his release.

According to the custom on the day, he had to carry an identity card. Thus no innkeeper upon knowledge of his past will allow him, a dangerous felon, to spend the night under his roof. For days, he wanders the village streets seeking shelter against the weather until a kind bishop has compassion for him.

That night Jean Valjean lies in his first comfortable bed, pretending to be asleep until he is sure that the bishop had drifted off. He rises quietly, rummages through the cupboards for the family silver or valuables, and then creeps off into the darkness.

The next morning a few policemen, with Valjean in arm, knock on the bishop's door. They have caught the scoundrel making of with the silverware and are ready to put the criminal in chains for life. However, the bishop catches everyone by surprise with his response.

"So there you are!" he blurts out to Valjean. "I'm delighted to see you back. Had you forgotten that I gave you the candlesticks as well? They are silver too and are worth a good 200 francs. Did you forget to take them?"

Valjean's eyes express what his words could not.

"Valjean is no thief," the bishop assured the gendarmes. "This silver is my gift to him."

When the policemen withdraw their grip on Valjean, the bishop hands over the candlesticks to his guest, now even more lost for words. "Do not forget, do not ever forget that you have promised me to use the money to make yourself an honest and better man."

The power of the bishop's act, defying every human instinct for revenge, even when he had the perfect opportunity, changes Valjean's life forever. A raw and naked encounter with forgiveness melts the granite walls of his soul. How does it end? Valjean keeps the candlesticks as a reminder of forgiveness and as a memento of grace and then dedicates himself to helping others in need.

However, forgiveness is often a two-edged sword as was in Hugo's novel. A detective named Javert knows no law but justice, and stalks Jean Valjean mercilessly over the next two decades. The more Valjean seems to be transformed by forgiveness, the more the detective is driven by an insatiable apatite for retribution. When Valjean eventually saves Javert's life (prey showing grace to the pursuer), the black-and-white, dog-eat-dog world of Javert begins to crumble. Unable to come to terms with forgiveness which goes against his instinct and logic and unable to find any corresponding grace within him, Javert jumps off a bridge into the river.

Justice has a good, righteous, logical, and rational kind of power but forgiveness holds its own extraordinary power which reaches beyond law and beyond justice. The grace shown through forgiveness is strangely unworldly, transforming and supernatural.

The questions stand—Are we capable of forgiving and showing love to the people around us even if they have hurt or let us down by not being perfect? Can we forgive them and love them because there are no perfect people in the world and because we hold the power to do so?

Principle—Mostly I cannot choose whether or not I suffer; I have in the past and I will to some degree in the future. But I can choose to not let suffering make me bitter, revengeful, less loving, and stuck.

- I will no longer focus on how I can avoid being hurt. Instead I will say to myself, "How can I, even in the midst of suffering choose to be more alive and loving?"

- Magnanimous forgiveness like that offered Valjean by the bishop will cost me something but I now accept that it opens the door for a miracle of transformation—both for the guilty party and for me.

- Who are my "others" that I need to forgive?"

— CHAPTER FOURTEEN —

HOW DO I KNOW IF I HAVE TRULY FORGIVEN?

HOW DO I KNOW IF I HAVE TRULY FORGIVEN?

I used to think that because I still felt the hurt when I heard that song, still felt the anger when I recalled that conversation, still cried when I remembered, and still needed to talk about it, perhaps I had not truly forgiven.

But I soon learned that forgiveness is not a feeling. Our memories however, are intricately linked to our feelings and so the marks of our journey that have etched their way into our soul will always be a part of who we are. They can either become our weakness or our strength.

After our decision to forgive or be forgiven, it is not only natural but it is crucial that we talk about it with trusted friends. Why?

- First, it draws out any denial, white washing, overexaggeration, lingering anger, and blame-shifting.
- Second, it calls it as it is. Naming an offense removes the mystery and cover-up and disarms its power over us by bringing it out into the open and facing it.
- Third, speaking about it keeps us accountable to those significant others in our life for the next season of change that confession and truth must bring.
- Fourth, it allows our ears to hear what our mouth is saying about us and others. It's often then that we begin to see reason and give voice to our own character and thoughts. It is also the beginning of establishing new mind sets as we retrain our brain to hear and respond to

our new information and decisions—creating our new kind of normal.

Speaking about our experiences is helpful for us and can also be very helpful to others who can learn from our mistakes, draw from our wisdom, and receive empathy from us as people who know and understand.

However, there is a difference between speaking about our experiences and continually bringing them up!

We spoke earlier about not confusing forgiveness with denial which is in essence burying offenses alive. Just as harmful is convincing ourselves and others that we have forgiven, but we still have an irresistible urge to keep digging up the past. Everyone's experiences (funnily enough) will find common ground with ours—except that ours will always be worse! They should hear about what happened to us! This is neither helpful nor healing.

I find myself mostly listening when life stories are shared. But when I speak, it comes from a place of personal forgiveness and healing. I don't have an urge to share my story or validate my misery. But when I do I am always surprised to find it laced with grace and seasoned with forgiveness—both from that which I have received and from that which I have given.

- How does that look? Dignified.
- How does that sound? Like heaven has found its way to my earth.
- How does that feel? Like the sting has been taken out of the bite.
- How do I see it? As a fresh beginning.
- What does it do? Encourages others.
- Where does it move me? Forward.

This is not a personal boast but a testimony of the supernatural touching the natural and changing the look of life altogether. It is testimony of the power of a choice—no offense is unforgivable unless we make it so. Use your power wisely.

There's no doubt about it, some of our experiences will leave us with a scar that will vie for our attention as we recall scenes, places, and people. Initially, we will cover each one and care for them, especially if they are raw, recent, and weeping.

Over time, we might scratch it when it itches and rub it when it hurts; but like any wound, our expectation should be that it will require less of our attention and be less debilitating as we apply the right healing balms at the time they are needed.

The forecast for a broken bone should be that we will have good to normal use of that part of our body if we see a doctor, have an x-ray of the area to have it assessed, wear a cast or support for the due time, allow it time to heal, and then gently exercise it back to recovery. As I have already said, bones can become stronger in the places they were broken. The same is true of broken hearts.

WHERE DOES RECONCILIATION FIT?

True forgiveness finds its secret rest in reconciliation. But here's what the dictionary defines reconciliation as—*to pacify or make peace with; to bring to agreement; to make or prove consistent.* For instance, a divorced couple can be reconciled and remain apart or be happily remarried when they have come to places of resolve and peace—with each other, with their children, and with their circumstances.

In a human sense, if reconciliation means a relationship is restored or renewed it's a bonus but reconciliation is not conditional on that happening.

The true meaning of the word finds its ultimate roots in the extraordinary act of God reconciling himself to the world. In an act of sacrificial forgiveness, he made peace possible again with a largely rebellious and unrepentant people.

His death closed the gap caused by sin, pacifying, and making peace and an agreement with humanity, while making relationship only a heartbeat away. When a person chooses to become a Christ-follower, he or she is responding to God's act of reconciliation.

Have you heard of people on their death beds desiring to "make their peace with God"? Although they didn't find the need for him in life, they suddenly find the need for him in death! Although they may not be putting it into fine language, they are seeking the peace that comes from knowing the debt is cancelled and the relationship is restored. The only sadness in leaving it until the desperate end is that their life will have missed many of the ripple-effect benefits that only forgiveness can bring.

WHEN LAUGHTER COMES

At the time of writing this book, a good friend emailed from oversees to share her heart with me regarding the recent passing away of her mother. She bannered her essay with "I know this is going to be helpful when you talk to others about this subject" and so with her permission, I share some of it with you.

As she briefly described her growing up years, she generalized with words like: "we were not well cared for"; "we never heard the words I love you"; and "my mother didn't seem to want to be a mother."

Reading between the lines painted an all too familiar picture of neglect, unnatural competition, insecurity, and resentment between parent and child. Add to that the disability of her father which caused him to be bound to a wheel chair from her earliest memories and the growing control and manipulation it fuelled in her mother, my friend could not recall any happy childhood memories.

Finally, at the tender age of seventeen, she escaped the prison of emotional abuse and left home for good. She had no plan, no money, and no regrets. It was a case of "anywhere but here."

I almost felt like an intruder as she led me on an intimate journey of her own personal experience of forgiveness. Time took her through marriage, motherhood, and a wildly uncommon move, near retirement age, to work with overseas aid.

Eventually a not unexpected word came through a phone call one afternoon announcing that her aging and frail mother had passed away. She described an instantaneous joy that filled her body and a strange sense of completion. She was not explaining her response through guilt or relief but rather through bewilderment at having lived out her purposed filled and happy life anyway.

Hers was not a macabre, "I'm glad she's gone" type of glee and I began to understand more as she went on. "I literally felt a dark cloud lift from my life and yet I had not been under my mother's influence nor controlled by it since childhood. I felt a heavy load lift from my shoulders although I had resolved not to assume personal responsibility for my mother's choices many years before." What was this feeling?

And then she said it, "I laughed." And at first glance, we may ask who could be so callous to laugh at the news of a mother's death?

The ancient poet expressed it something like this. *All I know is; forgiveness doesn't come with instructions but finds its expression through individually fashioned hearts.*[32]

My friend continued. "I laughed at the freedom I had—not that it was new as if it had been granted to me at the news of her death; no, I had it years before her death. You see, I chose while still a young woman not to live trapped by my past. No one taught me, it just sat better with my heart. Now I was laughing at the freedom that had been mine for most of my adult life! I felt like I had already won and that, now she was gone, I didn't have to think about the giants I had to face. I laughed with a grateful heart that my own children will have their own stories of forgiveness but they will have lived with the example and miracle of a mother forgiven and forgiving.

"I laughed with relief that many years ago I had loosed the grip of rejection; bitterness had relinquished its power and resentment had not been able to keep me prisoner. I had lived a free woman and my husband and children have reaped the rewards and legacy that such liberty can afford.

"I had forgiven my mum many years earlier. I had decided not to put conditions on my forgiveness, knowing that if I did my inner peace would be reliant on the decisions of the one who hurt me and disappointed me. I made a choice. I did what I knew to do. As far as I was concerned, for me, there were no wasted years.

"I also put my forgiveness faith in action. Over the years, I visited her as often as was geographically possible. I called and wrote. She rarely responded but I did so expectant and not conditional on her changing. I didn't do it for approval but I changed me. I knew I had.

"I was also able to lead her to meet her God. I assisted her in making her peace with her heavenly father. She was reconciled to him and reconciled to me. We had peace. Not best friends but peace. Not all the questions answered, but peace.

My girlhood picture of mother-daughter love, mentorship, and companionship did not happen but reconciliation did. And this would have to be enough.

"The expectation I had for mum was the same as the expectation I had for myself—it was high but anything better than what we initially had would be high, so it was also realistic and it was possible. I believe after this life the picture for us will be different. What we missed here we will live there."

Principle—No offense is unforgivable unless I make it so.

- I know I have forgiven because I haven't buried things but instead, found a trusted few with whom I can share my hurts, inner most thoughts, views, and feelings.
- I know I have forgiven because my satisfaction now comes more from forecasting my future than it does from replaying my past.
- I know I have forgiven, not because I have followed some sort of forgiveness formula but because my heart confirms that I have done all I knew to do when I had the time to do it.
- I know I have forgiven, not because my life is now picture perfect but because I know the meaning of reconciliation.
- I know I have forgiven because I am open and teachable knowing it's not too late to begin afresh.

"And I cried, but these were the tears that only forgiveness can release. Deb, this forgiveness power is the best-kept secret. We need to tell people this."

I just did! Thank you, friend, you continue to be an example to me.

— CHAPTER FIFTEEN —

RESTORATION—
BETTER THAN NEW

RESTORATION— BETTER THAN NEW

I love the lifestyle TV shows where experts move into someone's house and totally restore it. I love the transformation that a good renovation can bring to any home. I love the human capacity to see what is not yet and then set about making it happen. The eye of imagination is unique to us humans.

And I love the look on the owner's faces when they return to see their old home looking better than new! Imagine living in one of the shabbiest houses on the street yesterday and then living in one that turns heads today!

How can restoration be better than new? For a start, the old materials are replaced with new materials. Dated designs are superseded by innovative, attractive and functional ones. Brush strokes introduce color schemes that once belonged to another era into the here and now. The needs of a growing family are considered in the renovations until the negative and restrictive characteristics no longer define the home.

I have a bit of a fetish for chairs and I have restored a few old ones in my time. (A once cheap and therapeutic pastime for a single mum!) I picked up one pair of dining chairs from a small country town for a ridiculously low price. Dated in the forties, they had to be stripped of the old varnish and well sanded back to the original wood grain. From each chair, I removed the old seat with its split and cracked leather cover. Then I removed the old horse, hair padding, and wire springs. Each chair was revarnished and then padded with foam and a sturdy timber seat replaced the springs and straps. I then covered them with a fabric that blended with my interior and voila! I had the benefit of the old with their charm, their uncommon design, and their uniqueness but I had created something sensational after their modern and contemporary makeover. You will never find chairs quite like these!

My chairs had been restored to usefulness, function, and aesthetic value. I chose not to restore them to their former glory because I didn't actually see any glory in that look. Restoration for me had to look different, it had to suit my taste and desires; it had to look like my dreams; it had to be better than what I started with.

In the introduction, I asked if you had ever cried out within yourself or to God, "Please take me back to where it was all okay, right before it all went wrong." If you have cried something like that, then I have fantastic news for you!

God does restoration like we do restoration. When God does a work of restoration in our life, he doesn't have us looking, talking or acting like we did before.[33]

It seems that, in God's thesaurus, restoration is a synonym for promotion. So it makes perfect sense that our life will look different. Remind yourself of this when the unfolding and direction don't quite match the ideal picture you had envisaged. Learn to trust God's brush strokes.

The Bible is full of themes, language, and stories of people's lives where restoration resulted in elevation, promotion, transformation, and new beginnings. Where the dictionary describes restoration as reinstating or bringing back to the original state, God sees restoration as transformation to a higher state!

A couple of years into my new kind of normal, the story of a small group of fishermen crossing a lake captured my attention. It is the famous story of Jesus calming the wind and the sea.[34]

Jesus had suggested to a small group of disciples that they head east of Jordan to Gadara. It wasn't too far away by land but he chose to get there by sea. I realized after I had finished reading about their transit details to Gadara that these were not meaningless details, nor was it only of historical relevance for his companions.

There was a message of hope tucked into these boat boys' journey that would lift my sights and the level of my expectation and consequently impact my life from that day forward.

> *In choosing the sea route, Jesus gave these men*
> *a chance to know, beyond doubt, that he was*
> *Lord of terra firma and the safety of the known and*
> *also that he was Lord of the sea, the storms*
> *and the unknown.*

No sooner had they set out than a great storm suddenly blew up. That the men were afraid says something of the magnitude of the conditions as these men were old sea dogs. They were experienced fishermen who would have encountered every type of weather pattern and who were skilled at reading the signs; but not this day. This storm blew up from nowhere.

They may have expected that traveling with Jesus would secure a favorable voyage and a safe passage. (Christians still expect this to be so today!)

The storm raged and Jesus slept through it. The poor scared disciples thought they were all about to drown and dismally concluded that things were about to get worse. They awoke Jesus by yelling their cries for him to save them! They believed he could. I believe that this day it was both their language of fear and of desperate hope!

So he awoke! And he answered their cries for help. First though, he gently rebuked them for their anxious fear and lack of faith and trust. He reminded them that he was near and that he was trustworthy. This is our God of grace. Then He rebuked the wind and calmed the waves. This is the God of our circumstances. What he can do in us he can also do for us.

How effectually was this done? The story concludes with a description of conditions on the lake. Now *"there was a great calm."* The sea didn't revert to its original condition. It didn't even revert to an expected condition after such a storm. There were no fretful, confused, or disturbed poststorm waters but rather an immediate change to a lake far calmer than before the storm. These fisherman-turned-disciples, though long acquainted with the sea, had never in all their lives seen a storm transformed into such perfect calm. This had all the marks and signature of a miracle on it!

When Jesus awoke and answered his friends, he did so for all the aching dilemmas of man. Where is God in my storm? Where is God when I hurt? Where is he when I'm afraid? Where is he when I don't know the way? Right here; listening, caring, healing, and restoring. That's where.

> **Principle—The dictionary describes restoration as reinstating or bringing back to the original state; whereas God sees restoration as transformation to a higher state.**
>
> • Jesus has not been asleep during the events of my life; my calling out to him doesn't fulfill some sort of heavenly need in him but rather invokes his presence, invites his leadership, and confirms to me his nearness and trustworthiness.
> • Knowing and believing this, I will now give him the storms that I need him to calm.
> • I now ready myself to move past an old "Okay" and into a heavenly restoration of my life.

MY RESTORATION

For seven years, I raised my sons and my expectations. In the seventh year we prayed two prayers. First, we agreed together about the house we wanted to live in and the suburb that would suit us. We detailed both our needs and desires on a list that the boys kept on their bedroom mirrors. And then we thanked God that he is our restorer and provider. We thanked him when things were tough and money was tight.

Our list kept us preparing for the future season and our sights on better days. We cleaned out cupboards but kept those things we considered necessary for the next chapter of our journey. I taught the boys to cheer for the wins, victories, and promotions of friends and family in our world and defy the gravity pull of self-pity when things didn't seem to be moving for us.

Second, and very privately, I prayed another consistent prayer. Included in my thanks, my prayers for family, work, church, and the needs of others was a cameo of my own personal seasonal alertness.

Each afternoon as I walked our dog I would simply pray, "Lord, find me a husband like you found a wife for Isaac." You see, Isaac was the long-awaited son of the aging but faith-filled Abraham and his postmenopausal wife, Sarah. God had promised them a son through whom all the nations of the world would be blessed; the line through which the son of God would come to restore people to God. And so the couple waited.

Did Sarah rearrange the tent, visit maternity shops, plan baby showers? Probably, but she also watched the wallpaper fade, blew out a decade of birthday candles and still had no son.

That is, until a stranger paid them a visit confirming God's promise of a son, telling them they had better choose a name. God was about to change the number of names on their Medicare Card, change the way they would define "impossible," and most importantly, change the way they would understand trusting him. And as predicted and promised, Sarah gives birth.

This child was special, so when he was grown and of marriageable age, the custom of the day was to choose a suitable bride. She would have to be amazing.

She would have to share the same core values and believe in the same God. Abraham would have to be entirely pleased with her as a wife for his beloved and long-awaited Isaac and so would have set about detailing all the qualities and prerequisites this young woman might display. Then he sent his most trusted and seasoned servants out of the foreign land, he was in to the land of his fathers to bring back a wife for Isaac.

The mission was accomplished. The beautiful, well-brought up, and sweet Rebekah was the perfect match for Isaac. We can read the story for ourselves in the Book of Genesis chapter 24.

Like Abraham, I specified and detailed the husband I did not know yet. He would have to be amazing. I prayed that his core values would align with mine. I prayed about his character and for protection over it. I prayed for wisdom in his business decisions. I prayed about his spiritual growth and sharpness in his perceptions. I also prayed that God would be teaching me, preparing me, and honing me for this divine fit.

The point of my prayer was two-fold. One, I did not want to go looking for someone I believed God had set apart for me. I was not confident of my prior frame of reference and felt vulnerable in my state of singleness. Two, if someone whom I trusted and for whom I had great respect brought this man into my radar, I would pay attention. And this is just what happened.

Great friends and colleagues literally brought Philip into my world. Not too strangely, he also had a list. The "she" on his list was me. Ten months later, we were married. The boys reminded us in our first year of marriage that the list they had glued to their mirrors in all its detail was in fact realized in the house we now live in and own. Sharing our private lists together was a witness of our personal growth and resolve of core values . . . refined in the fires of pain and honed in the hands of God.

To say that God is a restorer in our English language somehow sounds ordinary and downplays who he is and what he does. We have not had our prior life with all its difficulties restored to us but rather we have experienced a restoration and a renovation transforming our lives to look like a dream come true!

Principle—Jesus is with me in my storm. He is trustworthy. He is a God of grace. I will "awaken" him so that he can rebuke the wind and calm the waves crashing around me. I give him the freedom to be the God of my circumstances.

- I refuse to settle for a standard restoration of things now broken. Rather, I eagerly anticipate a "better than" transformation.

- I accept responsibility for my part, and now ready myself for restoration, renovation, and promotion in my life.

- I refuse to allow anything to disract me, including the fierceness of the storm around me.

— CHAPTER SIXTEEN —

AFFIRMING LIFE

AFFIRMING LIFE

You may think it strange that in a book on forgiveness I have spoken a lot about acknowledging our Plan A and raising our expectation for a brighter future (one that lines up with our secret dreams and desires.) The reason is that I just can't separate forgiveness from the idea of a fresh beginning. The two go hand in hand!

When we truly grasp the concept of a forgiveness attitude, life translates into very different questions. We STOP asking ourselves why something happened and START asking how we will respond and what we intend to do now that it has happened . . . questions that open the doors to our future. The focus is removed from the event and back to us. We are then rightly positioned to use our unique power of moral freedom, choice, and change.

To write a book about how much I hurt and then add salt to injury by suggesting you try forgiveness would not be convincing or helpful to anyone. I knew this would have to be a book affirming life and affirming God's big YES over your life.

I was walking through the city of Melbourne along busy Swanson Street on my way home as a University student one afternoon when a small boy, around four years of age, ran to me, and clung to my legs. He was lost and frantic to find his mother. There is always good police presence in the city and I was only meters away from a kindly policeman. The little boy's mother was quickly located equally frantic to find her son.

When the policeman asked the boy why he clung to me, the lad answered, "She had a YES face." I think what he meant was that I looked like I would say yes before I would say no, that I would comfort before I would scold, that I would receive before I would turn away. I will never forget the honor the little boy bestowed on me that day. I had clung to God and discovered his YES face many years before and it had sustained me and carried me through some lost and frantic days.

One of Jesus's many YES statements was that he came into the world so that we may have abundant life. When he said that, he added a glorious adjective. It wasn't just to be an ordinary life. That adjective abundant translates variously *superabundance, excessive, overflowing, surplus, over and above, more than enough, profuse, extraordinary, above the ordinary, more than sufficient.*[35] A healthy and helpful question for us to ask ourselves regularly is . . . Are we creating room, margins, and space for such a life? The way we see our life (not just the events of life but our whole life) determines our destiny and influences the destiny of others.

However, before Jesus declared this mouth watering promise, and with the same breath, he said, "The thief does not come except to steal, and to kill, and to destroy . . ."[35]

I have known this thief. You have known him too. I battled with him through sleepless nights, dark days, through loss, tragedy, heart break, insult, and shattered dreams. There were times when I dared to believe in the abundant life promised and I fought; there were other times when I believed the thief and gave up. What I believed about my life began to shape my life. It shaped how I valued relationships, spent my money, used my talents, invested my time, and reflected God to the world around me. How is your life shaping up?

The great thing about Christ is that he came to earth in defense of life. He opposed any action, force, decision, or person that might diminish it in any way. He was constantly in trouble with teachers of the law and the religious leaders who interpreted the scriptures in a way that big-noted and empowered themselves but removed grace that would help to empower others.

Following his pattern, he calls us to a life of doing everything in our power to enhance the lives of people around us.

He calls us to defend life and lift the sights and hopes of others; assisting them to defy the gravitational pull of the ordinary, of second best and of Plan B.

TWO RESPONSES

At high school, I read two poignant accounts of two different people who survived Nazi persecution and the Holocaust of World War II. The two authors, Elie Wiesel and Corrie ten Boom, expressed two radically different responses to address the human cry of "How could God let six million Jews be savaged and suffer so horribly?"

I had watched documentaries on the events of the Holocaust and seen the award-winning film Schindler's List but none affected me so much as the book *Night* by Elie Wiesel.[36] Elie spent his teenage years in one of history's most horrifying chapters.

Elie saw all the Jews in his village herded together, stripped of their possessions, and squeezed into cattle cars where almost one third of them died. The first night this train pulled into Birkenau, Elie describes coils of ominous black smoke billowing from a massive oven and, for the first time, he experienced the smell of burning human flesh.

"Never shall I forget that night, seven times cursed and seven times sealed. Never shall I forget the smoke. Never shall I forget the little faces of the children, whose bodies I saw turned into wreaths of smoke beneath a silent blue sky. Never shall I forget that nocturnal silence which deprived me, for all eternity, of the desire to live. Never shall I forget those moments which murdered my God and my soul and turned my dreams to dust. Never shall I forget these things, even if I am condemned to live as long as God Himself. Never." [37]

Elie Eiesel's books roll out like a foreboding drum beat a tone of hopeless tragedy expressing like a physical reality that God is dead. The God of love and tenderness, mercy, and comfort; the God of Abraham, Isaac; and Jacob . . . dead. One interviewer of Elie described him as a man like Lazarus—raised from the dead yet still a prisoner stumbling within the grim confines of shameful corpses.

I think there is a tendency for us to identify with Elie and remain overwhelmed by tragedy. After such an ordeal, after such extreme human horror, how does one begin living again? How do words like "love," "hope" and "happiness" take on new meaning? And could anyone be so numb to his grief to suggest the character building qualities of suffering?

As I sit and write this I am acutely aware that I am underqualified to write about suffering or the extent of humanity's suffering when all I can boast of right now is a little chronic sinus trouble and the need for a good massage from sitting behind a computer. But I do know that one response elevates humanity to become the accuser making God the accused. As a result, he had nothing left but loneliness; an odd sense of being greater and stronger than the Almighty maybe, but still loneliness.

The other book I read was called The Hiding Place by Corrie ten Boom.[38] She recounts the same horror and human violations in her true story of surviving massive persecution. Interestingly, Corrie was not even a Jew but was driven to a death camp in Germany for aiding Jews. Although her book is not so graphically detailed as Elie, she describes the sting of the whip, the pangs of starvation, watching her sister die, the murders around her, the black void of disappearing virtue, and of a world of pure evil. Throughout her account, Corrie asks some of the same questions that Elie asks and sometimes her anger also rages against God.

But there is another element to Corrie's story that remains untenable or almost shallow to some secular views—and that is her underscored hope, faith, and victory. Woven through the story are little accounts of miracles, acts of sacrifice, and like golden threads, compassion binds this true story together as Corrie and her sister Betsie steadfastly trust in a God who sees them and cares.

I must admit, my first reaction was to warm to Elie's story as though some dark force was nudging me toward despair and away from life and hope. Although I entirely identify with Corrie's journey and believe in her God of absolute love, it was as if standing tall beside Elie as God's accuser was more noble in the face of human evil than standing small beside Corrie in a simplistic posture of faith.

I do not believe God condemns us in these moments of unanswered questions, despair, doubt, and unbelief. His death on the cross drove into earth the identification of cruel, inhumane, and senseless suffering. Only hours before this moment, Jesus asks if this cup of suffering could be passed from him; if there was any other way God's plan for humanity could be accomplished.

And then again, on the cross he cried out, "God my father, why have you forsaken me?" The full range of anger, fear, despair, and abandonment described in Elie's *Night* is also present in the Christian message. Jesus can fully identify with a suffering world and with the collective and individual pain of all humanity.

ALIVE BY BIRTH, LIVING BY CHOICE

I once heard a pastor speak about "despair's martyrs." We have heard of God's martyrs—people who have died with convictions of steel, a resolve in their belief in God, and a stand for the Christian message.

But the forces of disbelief and despair have their own martyrs too; people who weaken or shatter other people's faith in God and in the world. If the death of a teenager or the terminal illness of a child (for instance) leaves us blaming God, bitter, and less able to affirm life and the world's goodness, then we have become a "despair martyr." We have become a witness against God, against a meaningful moral order, against life, against hope. In so doing, we disempower rather than empower the lives of people around us. Human tragedies kill, but they do not have to kill a belief in life, faith, and dreams.

It isn't the circumstance of the tragedy but our reaction to it that causes us to be a witness for or against God; for or against life. Our reactions either affirm or neutralize life; they either enhance or disempower people, and they either make room for abundant life, or they restrict, downsize, and deny it.

If suffering or pain can cause us to explore the limits of our capacity for love, compassion, and selflessness; if it leads us to discover sources of consolation and faith that we never knew before, then we make the person, circumstances, or event behind the suffering an affirmation of life rather than a rejection of it.

I choose to live with the conviction that I am one of God's martyrs—not that I have tasted death nor intend having to before my natural time mind you! But having known physical and emotional rejection, abandonment, pain, loss, hardship, and crisis, I choose to reflect God's goodness and my belief in the world at large. I choose life. It is better for me. It is better for my children. And perhaps not strangely, my world becomes a bigger, brighter, and a safer place; people are attracted to the fragrance of it, benefit by the generosity in it, leave encouraged by it and want to know God because of it. Mind you, it was this way when I still lived in a small rented town house, had a minimal income, drove an embarrassing car, and eating out meant going to McDonalds!

Remember life is about 80% attitude and 20% circumstance! It just means that our choice of attitude miraculously has a way of altering circumstance!

As we begin to propagate the abundant life through our responses, reactions, and reflections, we will truly begin to live it. How? Our face says yes. Our hand stays outstretched. Our heart stays soft. Our mind stays open. And we can receive from God all that he intended for us and our family.

Principle—Christ came to earth in defense of life. He opposed any action, force, decision, or person that might diminish it in any way.

- I realize that I have allowed events and people to disempower me or to diminish my life.
- I accept Christ's promise of an abundant life. I also choose to play my part by establishing new responses or behaviors that will help open the door to God and the goodness he has carefully and lovingly placed around me.
- I refuse and resist the urge to be a despair martyr.
- To emphasize my commitment to living abundantly, I choose to live for others, bringing the flavor and realities of abundance in to their world.

PLAN A

No one ever promised us a life free from hardship, pain, and disappointment. What we are promised is that we do not have to be alone in our suffering; that we are able to draw on a higher source . . . One who understands and one who is both outside of us and inside of us. We are offered the strength and courage needed to survive life's tragedies and then to thrive despite them. I have already written about the epic act that ensured each one of us could live out Plan A.

It is the story of forgiveness. It all starts and ends here. Jesus's death is the cornerstone of the Christian faith, the most important fact of his coming and none of us can ignore the confronting reasons for it. Throughout his life, he laid down a trail of pictures, hints, stories, and predictions that were mostly understood only after the events had happened.

His exuberant and confident words from the night before he died must have cruelly haunted his friends and family as they helplessly watched him writhe and twitch on the cross. What possible reason could there be for God to suffer such pain and for our faith to be based on such suffering?

I can think of two reasons. The first one is that it provided solution to the chasm that exists between God and sin. Jesus substituted himself as the ultimate sin penance before God. Forgiveness smashed the sin barriers between God and mankind. Because of this, we can receive this forgiveness and be connected to our heavenly father. Intimate relationship is possible. At that very moment, eternity springs to life in our spirit and the temporary becomes clearly defined from the eternal.

The second reason is the image Jesus left for the world, the most universally known and recognized symbol. I am refering to the cross . . . proof that God knows about pain. He died of a broken heart.

Philip bought me a most beautiful necklace as a gift . . . a cross glittering with tiny reflective crystals. It starkly reminds me of how far we stray from the raw reality of history and yet I wear it proudly as a symbol that stands unique among all religions of the world. Most religions have gods, but only one has a God who cared and loved us enough to become a man and to die that we could live. Only one can take us to his place of death and find an empty grave.

Dorothy Sayers said this: *For whatever reason God chose to make man as he is—limited and suffering and subject to sorrows and death—he had the honesty and courage to take his own medicine. Whatever game he is playing with his creation, he has kept his own rules and played fair. He can exact nothing from man that he has not exacted from himself. He has himself gone through the whole of human experience, from the trivial irritations of family life and the cramping restrictions of hard work and lack of money to the worst horrors of pain and humiliation, defeat, despair, and death. When he was man, he played the man. He was born in poverty and died in disgrace and thought it well worthwhile.*[40]

In the previous chapter, I wrote about the parallel road of suffering that the cross of Christ and humanity share. But Christianity takes one giant step further, one which has caused division, argument, and been a stumbling block to many over the years. It is the resurrection of Christ from the burial tomb—the moment of fulfillment, hope, new life, and victory when death itself is smashed and God's Plan A is revealed again to mankind.

God doesn't ask us to embrace a Mary Poppins world of "smile and the world smiles with you." He only invites us to trust his presence and his wisdom. He asks that we run to him and not from him when we bleed and hurt. It's a mysterious layer he asks us to add to our human experience but I think it comes from the equally mysterious experience that defeated sin and death on the cross.

— CHAPTER SEVENTEEN —

STAMPED WITH ETERNITY

STAMPED WITH ETERNITY

I conclude this book with the third reason for Christ's suffering. It is the point of hope for anyone who has suffered, needed forgiveness, or needed to forgive and it is also found here in the shadow of the cross. It is this matter of Christ's resurrection.

About 3,000 years of history and human drama spotlights and points to the bloody and cruel death of Christ. It might be the centre of the whole story but it is not the end of the story. That story has to end with the resurrection (which really isn't an end at all!).

After carrying his limp body from the cross and traditionally burying him in a dark tomb, Jesus was seen alive again! His disciples could hardly believe it but he came to them and let them feel his new body and touch the nail prints in his hands. Jesus brought us the possibility of an afterlife without the pain and hurt. All of our suffering, then, is temporary.

Today, some are almost embarrassed to talk about an afterlife. It seems too quaint, childish, and maybe cowardly or perhaps even the cheap way out. But Jesus was raised from death to life to offer us both the possibility of a new beginning here on earth and one which will continue with him through eternity.

All our questions regarding immortality and eternal youth come from the way God wired our brains when he made us in his image—for eternity.

Abraham Lincoln said, "Surely God would not have created such a being as man to exist only for a day! No, no, man was made for immortality."

If our time on earth was all there was to our life and purpose, then we should begin to live it up immediately! We shouldn't worry about forming our character, creating our goals, doing good, defining our values, remaining ethical, or being moral because we won't have to worry about consequences or legacies.

We could be totally self-indulgent because our actions would have no long-term repercussions—none that we would have to worry about anyway.

But death is not the end. Our life strikes a chord that vibrates through eternity.

> *One eroding distinctive of any age is short-term thinking. When all our plans and decision making are merely reactions to current issues and solutions to current feelings then we miss the long-term harvest of good planning.*

Someone once said, "If we fail to plan, we plan to fail." The Sydney Harbor Bridge was dressed with lights spelling the word "Eternity" during the 2000 Millennium festivities. This was a message to the world pointing beyond today; it signaled future, hope, heritage, and destiny.

What does eternity look like? It's a bit like asking what God looks like. It's hard to wrap our mind around something that is bigger than the human mind. Knowing God is an ongoing experience that is caught in our heart igniting our spirit to come alive to him.

Eternity is much the same. God has given us glimpses of it throughout the Bible but for him to give us a clear picture that we would not misunderstand would be a little like trying to explain the internet to a mouse!

But more than a destination, eternity is who we are:
- Stamped and sealed with the Holy Spirit of promise. (In him you also trusted after you heard the word of truth, the gospel of your salvation; in whom also,

having believed, you were sealed with the Holy Spirit of promise . . . Ephesians 1:13)
- Having eternal purpose. (. . . He has made everything beautiful . . . also he has put eternity in their hearts . . . Ecclesiastes 3:11)
- Eternal life. (For God so loved the world that he gave his only begotten son that whoever believes in him should not perish but have everlasting life. John 3:16)
- Resurrection power. (. . . that I may know him and the power of his resurrection . . . Philippians 3:10-11)
- Faith filled for things yet unseen. (Now faith is the substance of things hoped for, the evidence of things unseen. Hebrews 11:1)

We were made to live forever but what we get to choose is whether we live forever in the presence of our creator and father, or live on in his absence. Receiving forgiveness of sin through God's love for us determines our eternity.

Our today is the visible tip of the iceberg and our eternity is the rest we can't see below the surface. Its expanse is outside our time frames and dimensions. Eternity will be full, expressive, progressive, colorful, expansive, and seriously fun!

C.S Lewis captured the concept of eternity on the last page of his famous Chronicles of Narnia:

"For us this is the end of all stories . . . But for them, it was only the beginning of the real story. All their life in this world . . . had only been the cover and the title page: now at last they were beginning Chapter one of the Great Story, which no one on earth has read, which goes on forever and in which every chapter is better then the one before." [41]

So how does living with an eternity mindset change anything? For a start, God's purposes involve far more than just our few decades on earth. I thought living with Christ at the centre of my life was an opportunity of a lifetime until I realized it was an opportunity beyond my lifetime!

It is an earthly season that will eventually transition into the eternal season. In the Chapter about seasons, I wrote that each one carries within it the DNA for the next season. So it is with us and eternity. We will carry something of who we were, who we became and who we impacted into eternity.

With eternity in mind and God in our life, it is interesting how much smaller our issues become and how loosely we will hold onto our things. What becomes paramount is the common ground where we and God meet—our heart. It's the place where forgiveness is cultivated, where love grows, where faith takes root, and where hope springs to life.

Keeping vigilant watch over our greatest gift is our most significant responsibility. Precious things can be lost, spoiled, contaminated, shrunk, or ruined if we are careless or indifferent. A hardened heart is perhaps the worst vestige of a neglected heart.

But there is another element to guarding, protecting, and nurturing our heart. An ancient proverb encourages us to guard our hearts because out of them flow the "issues" of life.[42] A literal translation from the original Hebrew proverb includes the word "boundaries." Now that proverb takes on a whole new expanse and even urgency. Now it reads: Keep your heart with all diligence for out of it flow the "boundaries" of life.

If we view boundaries as the fence line enclosing our life, then we have absolute input over the boundary markers! The degree of concern we take for the nurture of our own heart will be directly proportional to the boundaries of our life. What comes out of our heart will deliberately or unconsciously restrict our boundary markers or will expand and increase our territory! We are challenged to ask—Which areas do I want to grow? What do I need to increase? What needs to expand to accommodate my vision? I am confident that you will agree with me in wanting our worlds to be expanded, generous, and large.[43]

OUR RESURRECTION

I probably read it a hundred times before I saw it. It is part of the resurrection story and, in the blinding light of that monumental occasion, I had been missing the detail that was put there just for you and me.

When the Sabbath was over, Mary Magdalene, Mary the mother of James, and Salome brought spices so that they could embalm the dead body of Christ. Very early on Sunday morning, as the sun rose, they went to the tomb. They worried out loud to each other, "Who will roll back the stone from the tomb for us?" They looked up ahead and saw that it had been rolled back (it was a huge stone) so they walked right in. They saw a young man sitting on to the side, dressed all in white. They were completely taken aback, astonished.

He said, "Don't be afraid. I know you're looking for Jesus the Nazarene, the one they nailed on the cross. He's been raised up; he's no longer here. You can see for yourselves that the place is empty. Now—on your way. Tell his disciples and Peter that he is going ahead of you to Galilee. You'll see him there exactly as He said."[44]

There it is. Tucked into that panoramic moment are two words . . . "and Peter." A few days before this moment, Peter had committed acts of betrayal and rejection against Christ (having bragged that he would never do such a thing.) All of heaven watched him fall over. Now, in this moment of resurrection, all of heaven is stooping ready to pick him up again.

God sends the divine heavenly courier to reinforce his heart: "Be sure to tell Peter that he is not left out and that I am thinking about him. Be careful to tell him that a mistake is not a cancellation; a failure is not a flop and that Plan A still stands. Tell him God understands doubt and he understands fear. Tell him God isn't giving him a second chance because God doesn't need Peter to prove himself. God is giving Peter a fresh beginning because Peter needs to forgive himself."

The resurrection is a celebration of fresh beginnings! It is hope for eternity and new vision for today. Peter, the uneducated Galilean fisherman-turned-disciple-preacher-writer took this message of fresh beginnings all the way to Rome where they eventually killed him for the privilege. If you have ever wondered what causes a man to be willing to be persecuted and then crucified upside down, maybe this will give you a clue.

Roadblocked? Stuck? Paralyzed by hurt? Forgiveness and a fresh beginning is a heartbeat away. In a world that advocates "Stuff it up and you're gone"; "It's now or never"; "Two strikes and you're out," it's surprising to find someone who will give us a fresh beginning, much less someone who will give it to us every day!

In Jesus, Peter found both and we can too. His compassion toward us renews itself daily and he keeps his word.[45]

If I have written the book I wanted to write, it should be igniting in you a passion, perhaps even an obsession that will inflame a new lifetime adventure of discovery, insight, growth, and contentment not found through any other means. It should stir in you a fascination with forward. But you are the deciding factor for the direction of your life. You will determine how your story will end—on the precipice of the cliffs of Stuckville or the threshold of forgiveness, freedom, and eternity.

My concluding thoughts for you are summed up in three lots of twelve phrases that express what living a lifestyle of forgiveness will look like when its truth has etched its way into your heart. This journey has been and will be uniquely yours but I hope these statements remind you of the liberating miracle of forgiveness and help give voice to the longing you have had to live an extraordinary life. They sum up all that has been covered throughout the book. They are for your reflection. I hope you make them yours.

Always choose life and life will always choose you—Your friend and sojourner, Deborah Candler.

May we, through the understanding of true love expressed in forgiveness, learn to love OURSELVES enough to:
- quit rehashing the past,
- stop blaming ourselves for past choices,
- leave what keeps us small,
- believe this is our time,
- trust our inner divine guidance,
- welcome joy,
- find that desires of the heart do come,
- meet our own needs and not call it selfish,
- stop believing that life is hard,
- know that we are valued and worthy of knowing God intimately,
- recognize our own goodness,
- live in Plan A.

May we learn to love OTHERS enough to—
- shift our line of grace,
- use our power wisely,
- offer what we want to receive,
- build a life on a fresh foundation,
- sow seeds of reconciliation,
- throw away our ammunition,
- cultivate a "yes" face,
- take responsibility for our feelings,
- navigate away from hurt and bad behavior,
- see deeper than the surface,
- affirm life,
- claim as a new self-definition "one who forgives."

And may we learn to love GOD enough to—
- look for every day miracles,
- allow his truth to emerge in our life,
- let ourselves fall into his embrace,
- practice words of trust (I believe, I am confident, I am not afraid.)
- anticipate the many disguises of grace,
- assume the posture of faith and surrender,
- stop blaming him,
- cultivate strength and courage,
- become his hands and feet to our world, • open ourselves to divine action and abundance,
- help him to help us,
- allow him to work our ends into beginnings.

For us this is the end of all the stories . . . But for them, it was only the beginning of the real story. All their life in this world . . . had only been the cover and the title page: now at last they were beginning Chapter One of the Great Story, which no one on earth has read, which goes on forever and in which every chapter is better than the one before.

C.S Lewis: The Chronicles of Narnia

© Deborah Candler 2008

END NOTES

Why so many translations of the Bible? This book contains many quotations from the Bible. I have intentionally varied the translations for two main reasons.

First, the Bible was originally written using 11,280 Hebrew, Aramaic, and Greek words however, the English translation only uses around 6,000 words. The divine nature of the scripture ensures that the theme is preserved but nuances and shades of meaning can be missed so it is always helpful to compare translations.

Second, we can easily miss the impact of many scriptures not because of translation but rather because we have become too familiar with them assuming we know what it says and so skip over them. Varied translations make use of corresponding English words and will often give a freshness to a well-known verse.

Sources

The two sources I have chosen to use are the New King James (NKJ) and the Message Bible (MB) translations.

New King James Version, Copyright © 1979, 1980, 1982 by Thomas Nelson, Inc. Used by permission. All rights reserved.

The Message: *The Bible in contemporary language* Copyright © 2002 by Eugene H Peterson. All rights reserved.

APPENDIX

1. C.S Lewis quote,
2. Isaiah 44:2 (MB)
3. John 3:1-2 (MB)
4. Mark 5:21-34 (NKJ)
5. Mark 10:46-52 (NKJ)
6. Ecclesiastes 9:11 (NKJ)
7. Genesis 8:22 (NKJ)
8. Genesis 1:1-31 (NKJ)
9. John 15:1-2 (NKJ)
10. 1Corinthians 2:9 (NKJ)
11. Hebrews 12:15 (NKJ)
12. Psalm 119:63 (NKJ)
13. Matthew 7:13-25 (MB)
14. Romans 12:2 (NKJ)
15. 2 Corinthians 10:3-5 (MB)
16. Luke 23:42-43 (NKJ)
17. Matthew 27:46 (NKJ)
18. Psalm 103:12 (NKJ)
19. 1 Corinthians 10:4-5 (NKJ)
20. Psalm 119:105 (NKJ)
21. Luke 15:11-32 (NKJ)
22. Romans 5:8 (NKJ)
23. Mark 11:25 (MB)
24. 2 Corinthians 12:9 (NKJ)
25. Mark 11:25 (MB)
26. Matthew 5:23-24 and
    Mark 11:25-26 (NKJ)
27. Matthew 18:21-35 (MB)
28. Matthew 6:9-13 (NKJ)
29. Jeremiah 29:11-12 (NKJ)
30. Matthew 26:69-75 and John
    21:1-14 (NKJ)
31. Luke 23:34 (NKJ)
32. Psalm 33:15 (NKJ)
33. 2 Corinthians 5:17 (NKJ)
34. Matthew 8:23-27 (NKJ)
35. John 10:10 (NKJ)
36. Elie Wiesel, Night (New York:
    Avon Books, 1969)
37. Elie Wiesel, Night (New
    York:Avon Books, 1969) P.9
38. Corrie ten Boom, The Hiding
    Place (Hodder and Stoughton
    and Christian Literature
    Crusade, 1976)
39. Proverbs 11:24 (MB)
40. Dorothy L Sayers, Christian
    Letters to a Post Christian
    World, (Grand Rapids, Mich:
    William B Erdmans Publishing
    Company 1969)
41. C.S Lewis, The Last Battle
    (New York: Collier Books,
    1970) 184
42. Proverbs 4:23 (NKJ)
43. Proverbs 11:24 (MB)
44. Mark 16:1-5 (NKJ)
45. Lamentations 3:22-23 (NKJ)